HOW TO GET THE MOST OUT OF THIS COURSE

SUGGESTIONS FOR GROUP LEADERS

We're deliberately not prescriptive, and different leaders prefer to work in slightly different ways, but here are a few tried-and-trusted ideas …

1. THE ROOM Encourage people to sit within the main circle – so all feel equally involved.

2. HOSPITALITY Tea or coffee and biscuits on arrival and/or at the end of a meeting are always appreciated and encourage people to talk informally.

3. THE START If group members don't know one another well, some kind of 'icebreaker' might be helpful. Be careful to place a time limit on this exercise!

4. PREPARING THE GROUP Explain that there are no right or wrong answers, and that among friends it is fine to say things that you're not sure about – to express half-formed ideas. If individuals choose to say nothing, that's all right too.

5. THE MATERIAL It helps if each group member has their own personal copy of this course book. Encourage members to read each session *before* the meeting. There's no need to consider all the questions. A lively exchange of views is what matters, so be selective. The quotations in blue are there to stimulate discussion and – just like the opinions expressed by the audio participants – don't necessarily represent York Courses' views or beliefs.

6. PREPARATION It's not compulsory for group members to have a Bible, but it might be helpful for at least the leader to have one handy. Ask in advance if you want anyone to lead prayers or read aloud, so they can prepare.

7. TIMING Aim to start on time and stick fairly closely to your stated finishing time.

8. USING THE AUDIO/VIDEO For each of the sessions, we recommend reading through the session in the course book, before listening together to the corresponding session on the audio material/watching the video. Groups may like to choose a question to discuss straight after they have listened to/watched a relevant track on the audio/video – but there are no hard-and-fast rules. Do whatever works best for your group!

9. THE TRANSCRIPT, included at the end of the course book, is a written record of the audio/video material and will be invaluable as you prepare.

RUNNING A VIRTUAL HOUSE GROUP AND SHARING AUDIO/VIDEO

To run your virtual group, use software such as Zoom or Google Meet, and use the 'Share Screen' function to share the audio/video with your group.

HOW TO DOWNLOAD THE AUDIO AND VIDEO

To access the downloadable videos that come with the course book, go to https://www.spckpublishing.co.uk/the-life-in-the-comma-york-courses-video. You can watch and download the videos there. To download the audio, go to https://www.spckpublishing.co.uk/the-life-in-the-comma-york-courses-audio and use the code TheLifeInTheCommaMP3 to purchase the audio for free on the site.

T0326665

The full list of available formats is as follows:

- Course book including transcript of video and access to video/audio downloads (paperback 978 1 915843 41 8)
- Course book including transcript of video and access to video/audio downloads (eBook 978 1 915843 42 5, ePub and Mobi files provided)
- Participants' book including transcript of video: pack of 5 (Paperback 978 1 915843 45 6)
- Participants' book including transcript of video (eBook 978 1 915843 44 9, both ePub and Mobi files provided)
- Video of discussion to support *The Life in the Comma*, available via the course book with access to audio and video downloads
- Audio book of discussion to support *The Life in the Comma* (audio/digital download 978 1 915843 40 1)

THE LIFE IN THE COMMA

Deepening our understanding of Jesus

An ecumenical course in four sessions

John L. Bell

CONTENTS

Introduction   v
Acknowledgements   vi

Sessions
Session 1   Advent – a time for the kids?   1
Session 2   The life omitted   8
Session 3   Unspoken in Advent   16
Session 4   A life of risk   25

Transcript
Introduction   33
Session 1   Advent – a time for the kids?   34
Session 2   The life omitted   42
Session 3   Unspoken in Advent   49
Session 4   A life of risk   59

INTRODUCTION

This Advent course may seem a little unconventional in that it does not centre on the Old Testament prophecies and the nativity narratives in the Gospels, not that these are excluded.

For long, I have felt a dissatisfaction with the two adjacent statements in the Apostles' Creed which are separated by a comma: 'Born of the Virgin Mary, suffered under Pontius Pilate.' Nothing is said about the life and ministry of Jesus. Yet Jesus did not simply appear on earth in order to be crucified, nor would he have been crucified if his life had been unthreatening.

I believe that, for our fullest celebration of the Christmas seasons, it is important to at least glimpse the larger Christ, not only the baby in the manger and the Saviour on the cross.

So, in the four sessions that follow, we will both question the 'routine' celebration of the seasons and ponder deeply the implications of the great event we call the Incarnation.

ACKNOWLEDGEMENTS

I would like to express my appreciation to Alison Barr, the commissioning editor, and to other staff of SPCK for their care and diligence in preparing this publication. Thanks also to Smitha Prasadam and Lauren Windle who engaged in the conversation recorded in the accompanying video and audio downloads.

SESSION 1
ADVENT – A TIME FOR THE KIDS?

GETTING TO KNOW YOU

Imagine that one day you were so curious about the background of a person you had recently befriended that you said to him or her, 'Tell me about your mother.' What would you think if your friend replied, 'Well, she was born in Manchester in 1954 and died in Preston in 2017'?

This would seem a rather curt and dismissive description of someone whom your friend presumably knew and loved. You might have been hoping for more information regarding your friend's mother – how many children she had, what her main interests were, whether she had pursued a life-long career, what were her most endearing or quirky characteristics. Basic information regarding her birth and death would seem almost dismissive or desultory.

So what about Jesus?

A CREDAL COMMA

In the Apostles' Creed, to which most Christians subscribe, Jesus' life seems to be reduced to a comma, sandwiched between the name of two notables:

'Born of the Virgin Mary
comma
suffered under Pontius Pilate.'
APOSTLES' CREED

This is echoed in several Christian hymns which, in alluding to the life of Jesus, make a seamless transition from the cradle to the cross.

Admittedly, the Creed also refers to Jesus' conception, and to his crucifixion, resurrection and ascension. But these seem like a list of events of profound spiritual significance divorced from any glimpse of humanity in the Saviour of the world. If the Apostles' Creed was your primary introduction to the Christian faith, it would hardly offer comprehensive information.

Have you ever thought about this?

'To be human is to be a narrative creature. From the earliest days of our lives, we understand that every story worth telling or worth hearing has a beginning, middle, and end.'
R. ALBERT MOHLER JR[1]

The Creed, of course, was never meant to be a potted biography of Jesus. It was a concise statement of faith in the Trinitarian God which took around four hundred years to formulate. It began to be used in public worship in the eighth century. But it is hardly an incentive to belief and discipleship.

'When we reach the point where the Creed no longer looks or sounds to Christian people like a declaration of the gospel, there is need, I believe, for some whistle-blowing and reassessment of what goes on. For in fact the Creed itself was born as an instrument of evangelism.'
J. I. PACKER[2]

A CHILD'S PERSPECTIVE

To know that Jesus was born and that he died is not enough. This was brought home to a priest I met in Nottingham some years ago. Her parish church was keen to make good links with the local state primary school. One of the ways in which this happened was the practice of the congregation to invite children in their third or fourth year to visit the church at Christmas and Easter.

On both occasions, members of the congregation would dress up as the principal characters in the nativity or Passion narratives, and locate themselves in different parts of the church. When the children came in, they were encouraged to wander round the various cameos and ask questions of the characters.

'I auditioned for the role of an angel in the nativity play at school. I didn't get it. I auditioned for Mary: I didn't get it. So I made up the character of the sheep who sat next to Baby Jesus.'
NICOLE KIDMAN[3]

Both the children and the adult volunteers enjoyed this way of engaging with the two main Christian festivals.

However, what made the priest question the efficacy of the practice was what happened one Holy Week when a class of children was lined up outside the church.

The teacher spotted a boy who had been required to repeat a year. He, therefore, had been at the church events before. She overheard him slightly bragging to the other boys around him in these words: 'I know what this is all about. They're going to tell us how the Romans killed the baby Jesus.'

What about Jesus' life?

POPULAR BELIEF

If you were to ask the generality of people in Britain who had some connection with the Christian faith what were the defining characteristics of Jesus, you might find three adjectives being used which don't feature very much in the Gospels.

They are *gentle, meek* and *mild*. These rather passive descriptors owe their popularity to hymns of a previous era, especially children's hymns, that talk about Jesus being gentle, meek and mild.

The word 'meek' is particularly problematic. In the sixteenth century, it meant 'humble'. But in today's world, if someone is called meek, the suggestion is that he or she is reticent or ineffectual.

'"Gentle Jesus, meek and mild" is a snivelling modern invention, with no warrant in the Gospels.'
GEORGE BERNARD SHAW[4]

In the ever-popular carol, 'Once In Royal David's City', Jesus' presumed defining characteristics become mandatory for his juvenile followers. Thus:

'And through all his wondrous childhood
he would honour and obey,
watch and love the lowly maiden
in whose gentle arms he lay.
Christian children all must be
mild, obedient, good as he.'
CECIL FRANCES ALEXANDER[5]

It is interesting to note that, for a Jewish boy, childhood continued until his Bar Mitzvah at the age of eleven or twelve. The only thing we know about Jesus' historical 'wondrous childhood' is that he ran away from his parents when they were returning from the Passover in Jerusalem. To be biblically accurate, perhaps these words should substitute these last two lines:

'Christian children must abscond
if of God they're truly fond.'

TWO ISSUES

We have to ponder two things. The first is that, if Jesus were as passive as the favoured descriptions suggest, why did he get crucified? Most people who have had their life terminated by public execution have lived lives which, in whatever way, were at least 'eventful'.

'The moment God is figured out with nice neat lines and definitions, we are no longer dealing with God.'
ROB BELL[6]

The second question must concern why adjectives such as gentle, meek and mild – which have little verification in the Gospels – have taken precedence over other descriptions such as charismatic, gregarious and incisive, which are much more easily substantiated.

Has there been a plot – conscious or unconscious – to try to soften Jesus and present him as overwhelmingly nice, non-controversial and easy-going? Is it an attempt to present him as the convenient Saviour we'd prefer, rather than the demanding Saviour whom God knows we need?

'Jesus Christ wants to be in his own person God's answer to the human condition.'
LEONARDO BOFF[7]

It is in the seasons from Advent to Epiphany that most people, in their childhood, are introduced to Jesus. Christmas is popularly referred to as 'a time for the kids'. The carols – especially those of Victorian and mid-twentieth-century origin – depict Jesus as the kind of child most mothers would worry about. His birth is a very silent affair (according to 'O Little Town of Bethlehem') and he never cries (according to 'Away in a Manger'). Add the seasonal embroidery of robins, little donkeys, mistletoe and fir trees and something of the starkness of the nativity is lost, as well as something of the normality of Jesus.

In contrast, consider this text written by a boy aged three and half in 2003:

'Father God, I love you
and your little Jesus.
I would like to kiss him
and give him a cuddle.
I would share all my toys,
and play lots of games with him.
Bob the builder we could play;
we would be the best of mates.'
ISAAC HUTCHINGS (AGED 3)[8]

Nor do the popular depictions of Mary do justice to her. Apart from interminably wearing blue, she is also as slim before birth as after. Years ago, in a Roman Catholic church in Glasgow, a group in the congregation worked at producing four contemporary murals to be displayed in sequence during the four Sundays in Advent.

All went well until Mary appeared, looking heavily pregnant. That depiction was regarded as an outrage to some.

THE AWKWARD TRUTH

It is interesting to discover from archaeological research that the birth of Jesus – far from being a risk-free, happy event – would have been cloaked in apprehension. According to Bruce Malina and Richard Rohrbaugh, one in three children died at birth as did one in four women giving birth. And of live births, a third were dead by the age of six. Pregnancy and babyhood were high-risk ventures.[9]

If such statistics were not published in the Gospels, then certainly Matthew (more than Luke) does not deny that the whole venture of God coming among us was fraught with peril. Joseph, as Matthew records, was not exactly over the moon to discover that his betrothed was pregnant. He was intent on terminating the engagement, had not God intervened to persuade him otherwise.

This episode must have been quite nerve-racking for Mary, because Jewish communities were not exactly sympathetic to women who had children out of wedlock. A Jewish man expected to marry a virgin, not wed a girl whose child was fathered by another suitor.

A further experience of insecurity is mentioned by Matthew with regard to how Herod, the regional monarch, was not best pleased to discover that a potentially rival king had been born. Out of either fear or bloody-mindedness, he orders a cull of Jewish boys aged three and under. Hence, the Holy Family flee their homeland and make for Egypt which – at least historically – was a country regarded as hostile to the Jews.

Is it odd or is it intentional that, in the celebration of Jesus' birth, the risk factors are downplayed in favour of attention being given to the more pleasing and popular aspects of the nativity?

FOR DISCUSSION

1. Has your appreciation of the Christmas story increased or decreased as you have got older? And if so, why?

2. Some information has been given regarding the risk factors in being pregnant and giving birth in first-century Palestine, as well as the need for the Holy Family to flee as refugees. Do you think that these less savoury elements of the story add to or subtract from its significance?

3. On a more general plane, do you feel that we tend to be surrounded by more passive images of Jesus than more realistic and demanding ones? If so, why?

SESSION 2
THE LIFE OMITTED

WHAT THE HYMNS TELL US

A decade ago, I was asked to give a lecture in St Martin in the Fields on the subject of 'Jesus in the Song of the Church'.

'Paul commands the Church to let the word of Christ dwell in us richly when we meet together, singing psalms, hymns, and spiritual songs. It seems clear here that style is not the important issue as much as the depth of content.'
KEITH GETTY[1]

'Hymns are the poetry of the people.'
JOHN BETJEMAN[2]

I researched the major denominational hymns which were published up until the mid-twentieth century in Anglican, Baptist, Methodist and Presbyterian churches, and was amazed to discover how little of the life of Jesus had been celebrated in song.

All traditions were united in a plenitude of material regarding the birth, death and resurrection of Jesus. Most traditions had songs of devotion to Jesus. But when it came to his life and ministry, it was as if the hymn writers and publishers followed the Apostles' Creed in subsuming thirty-three years in a comma.

Here is an extract of the findings:

The Church Hymnary of 1898:[3]
- 5 hymns on the advent, birth and epiphany
- 4 on the incarnate life
- 23 on Passion and death
- 12 on the resurrection

The English Hymnal of 1906:[4]
- 44 on the advent and birth
- 6 on the incarnate life

- 27 on the Passion and death
- 19 on the resurrection

Redemption Songs of 1900:[5]
- 6 on the advent and birth
- 0 on the incarnate life
- 32 on the Passion and death
- 6 on the resurrection

The people Jesus met, the things he said, the controversy he caused, the miracles he performed, the particular affection he had for women and marginalised peoples – all of these were ignored.

'"Jesus" was a name that was usually translated as, "Saviour," but now it is better translated as "Liberator." The Hebrew name is *Jesua*, which means "Yahweh is liberation".'
ERNESTO CARDENAL[6]

'Jesus as an historical personality distinguished himself from other religious personalities of his time by his friendly attitude to the outcasts of society.'
C. H. DODD[7]

One common hymn, 'O Sing a Song of Bethlehem', moved on to Nazareth in verse two and to Calvary in verse three.[8] It reflected the notion of 'the child born to die'. Not until Sydney Carter with 'Lord of the Dance' was there a popular song which attempted to celebrate his life, and even then the life is covered in two verses out of five.[9] This endorsed my belief that, if we only sing about Jesus' birth and death, we are dealing with aspects of his life which have no immediate bearing on our lifestyle. But if we sing of his life, which we are called to emulate, then we are informing ourselves about discipleship.

'As spiritual singers, slaves were not bothered about the chronological distance between the biblical era and their present. Operating on a sense of sacred time, they extended time backwards so as to experience an intimacy with biblical persons as faith relatives.'
KATIE GENEVA CANON[10]

'Christianity without discipleship is always Christianity without Christ. It remains an abstract idea, a myth which has a place for the fatherhood of God, but omits Christ as the living Son. Discipleship without Christ is a way of our own choosing. It may be the ideal way, but it is devoid of all promise. Jesus will certainly reject it.'
DIETRICH BONHOEFFER[11]

WHAT THE ARTWORK SUGGESTS

This selective representation of the life of Jesus is reflected in the iconography of the Church. To this end, it might be interesting to reflect on how physical depictions of Jesus, whether from childhood Bibles, Sunday school posters or stained-glass windows, have limited or increased our knowledge of him. How many can we remember which depicted Jesus as vigorous, determined and passionate compared with those which were predominantly pastoral?

'For where I found Truth, there found I my God, the Truth itself.'
AUGUSTINE, BISHOP OF HIPPO[12]

In the Kelvingrove Art Gallery in Glasgow, we have a painting of Jesus which is world-famous. It was purchased in the mid-fifties. Its selling price was in the region of £12,000 which managed to get whittled down to £8,500. Its purchase caused no small dissension in the city. Art students got up a petition demanding that the money be used to build an exhibition space for struggling artists. The cognoscenti in the art world said that it was kitsch and of little artistic merit. Protestants in the city complained it was a flagrant misuse of public money to purchase such a work from a dubious Spanish Roman Catholic artist.

It is now arguably the most treasured and valuable artwork the city owns.

The painting was *Christ of St John of the Cross* by Salvador Dali.[13] It is a crucifixion, but the view is not from the ground looking up at a wounded and dying saviour, with blood and the marks of scourging all over his body.

'It is not of this world, and yet it is, and that is how it should be.'
EDWIN MORGAN[14]

Instead, the view is from above, looking down on the beautiful, muscular and unblemished image of Jesus. Dali knew how most depictions of the crucifixion showed the cruelty of humanity in killing Jesus. But what he depicted was not a wretch being done to death, but the assassination of one in whom was the perfection of beauty, truth and love. This was not simply a man of sorrows acquainted with grief; this was the One in whom 'the fullness of God' lived and breathed.[15]

If I were to identify the pieces of creativity which influenced my own thinking about Jesus, they would be two pieces of drama five hundred years apart. One was a three-part performance in a London ballroom of the York Mystery Cycle. The first part dealt with the creation of the world, the second and third focused on the life and ministry of Jesus. These were electrifying pieces of drama, all the more so because they happened in the midst of the audience rather than on a stage. The blind man came tapping through the crowd with his stick and was healed among us; Jesus was physically captured and dragged away from engagement with us by Roman soldiers.

The other event was seeing *Godspell* for the first time at the Round House in Chalk Farm, with David Essex as Jesus. I was bowled over by the articulation of the text, directly taken from Luke's Gospel, which hitherto I had only read on the pages of my Bible or heard in church, spoken sometimes as if it were a chore rather than a privilege to give voice to the Gospel. But In *Godspell*, what had been black-and-white text became technicolour, not because the words were changed, but because they were spoken in direct speech as if every word mattered. All the frustration, all the emotion, and even the humour which was in Jesus became clear. Scales had fallen from my eyes.

'*Godspell* was not about whether Jesus was divine, in the way that *Jesus Christ Superstar* is. It was about what this character taught and how his lessons changed society.'
STEPHEN SCHWARTZ[16]

WHAT'S THE POINT?

'What's the point of all this?' you might be asking.

Rather than my answering that question, suppose I follow Jesus' tendency to respond to one question by raising another.

If we consider the world we live in today as objectively as possible, and were to make a list of the burning issues which affect everyone and not just people of faith, what would they be?

Judging by what makes headlines in the news, these are the most significant:

- The ecological health of the world
- Global insecurity – caused by ongoing military conflict
- Racism and multicultural societies
- Health and welfare provision
- Sexual politics and gender identity
- The disparity in wealth and power between the very rich and the poor.

'The world's richest 10% … anyone paid more than about $40,000 (£32,000) a year … are responsible for half of all global emissions, making them key to ending the climate crisis.'
DAMIAN CARRINGTON[17]

'Of the 100 largest economic entities in the world, 69 are corporations and only 31 are countries.'
GLOBAL JUSTICE[18]

There are other significant issues, and their importance will be differently rated by different people. Try in your group to put the above list of issues in order of importance (1 to 6) and see if everyone agrees.

If you were to point people who are suffering because of the injustices indicated above to the teaching of Jesus, would that be an easy thing to do?

If all we could say is, 'Believe in Jesus for he is the Saviour of the world. He was born at Bethlehem and he died for the sins of the world at Calvary', would that make any impact?

This is not to question or belittle evangelism, or to underestimate the importance of personal salvation. But personal salvation is not the same as the redemption of the world.

'The real issue isn't whether our generation is wearing enough bedazzled cross T-shirts; it's whether we are allowing the message of Jesus to root deeper than our wardrobe, blog posts, music playlists, tweets, and Facebook statuses. We've become a tribe of people who rank our faith in a measurement of likes, re-tweets, and memory verses. We need to up our game.'
JARRID WILSON[19]

'How much easier to write about safe topics such as love, courtship and marriage, rather than spend sleepless nights pounding the typewriter, writing about events and incidents that grip one's soul.'
EVELYN MIRANDA-FELICIANO[20]

Two of the most common texts used with regard to Jesus are:

'Behold, the Lamb of God, who takes away the sin of the world.'
JOHN 1:29, JUB

'For God so loved the world, that he gave his only Son,
that whoever believes in him should not perish but have
eternal life.'
JOHN 3:16, ESV

Both of these may be associated with receiving Holy Communion
and sometimes appear on Easter greetings cards.

But they do not appear in the Gospels in association with either
the institution of the Eucharist or the Passion narratives. The first
is a statement which John the Baptist makes when he sees Jesus
walking towards him on the river bank (John 1:29). The second
appears at the end of a conversation Jesus has with Nicodemus
(John 3:16). They have come from moments at the beginning of the
ministry of Jesus and have been associated with the end of his life.

We need to recapture the fullness of Jesus whose gospel is about
the wholeness of life and not just the religious elements. For in truth,
Jesus did not come to save the Church or Christians, but the world.

'I experience religious dread whenever I find myself
thinking that I know the limits of God's grace, since I am
utterly certain it exceeds any imagination a human being
might have of it. God does, after all, so love the world.'
MARILYNNE ROBINSON[21]

In the original Greek, the word for world is *cosmos*.

And he came not simply that he should save our souls, but that his
joy might be in us and our joy become complete.

FOR DISCUSSION

1. What were the dominant images of Jesus you inherited from
childhood?

2. Look at the picture of *Christ of St John of the Cross*. Do you find
it helpful that the beauty of Christ should be the focus rather than
the suffering?

3. Looking at the contemporary issues listed above, which of them do you feel is best addressed and which is the least addressed in the teaching of the Church? Why is this so?

UNSPOKEN IN ADVENT

There are some people in the cycle of stories we hear of at Christmas who are not referred to very often. Mary, Joseph, the shepherds and the baby Jesus tend to predominate. But these other less mentioned figures are not without their significance. Among other things, they introduce us to aspects of God's justice, dear to the heart of Jesus and important for the world today.

'I felt that I had been born anew and that the gates of heaven had been opened. The whole of Scripture gained a new meaning. And from that point on the phrase, "the justice of God" no longer filled me with hatred, but rather became unspeakable sweet by virtue of a great love.'
MARTIN LUTHER[1]

FORGOTTEN PEOPLE

The first four are skimmed over when we read the genealogy of Jesus in Matthew's Gospel. In chapter one there are forty named male ancestors from Abraham to Jacob, the father of Joseph, and only four named female ancestors. More peculiar is the fact that while Jews inherited their identity from their mother rather than from their father, the four named women were not Jewish. To some extent they point to an imperfect family tree; their children were not fully pedigreed.

Equally alarming, if we read their stories, is the fact that each of them had an unusual sexual history.

'Through Jesus' family tree, God puts his grace on display ... reminding us that he can do for us what we cannot do for ourselves: pick up broken pieces and put them together, take broken lives and make them whole, gather broken hopes and make them reality.'
JAMES MERRITT[2]

- Tamar, wife of Judah, was a Canaanite who dressed as a prostitute and seduced her father-in-law (Genesis 38).
- Rahab ran a brothel in Jericho, and was operative in enabling Joshua to invade her city (Joshua 2).
- Ruth, wife of Obed, was a Moabite who was encouraged by her mother-in-law to make herself available to a much older man (Ruth 3).
- Bathsheba, possibly a Hittite, was seduced into an adulterous relationship by King David (2 Samuel 11).

'Matthew lists Rahab as one of the ancestresses of the Lord Jesus Christ (Matthew 1:5), and that may be one reason why there was something about free-wheeling ladies with warm and generous hearts that he was never quite able to resist.'
FREDERICK BUECHNER[3]

These four women are in Jesus' family tree, and I want to suggest that their place there symbolises two things. The first is the way in which women were often regarded as accessories, but in Jesus' ministry they become essential. The second is that they also symbolise the ambivalent relationship the Jewish people had with foreigners – another class of people important to Jesus.

'Jesus abandoned the usual solidarity of the family in order to make "those around him" into his "brothers and sisters and mothers."'
ALBERT NOLAN[4]

WOMEN FIRST

Here are the names of some more women who appear in the Hebrew Scriptures:

- Puah
- Hagar
- Jael

- Abigail
- Jochebed
- Zelophehad's daughters
- Rizpah
- Deborah

How many of them are familiar to you in more than name?

'I look forward to the day when women with leadership and insight, gifts and talents, callings and prophetic leanings are called out and celebrated as Deborah, instead of silenced as Jezebel.'
SARAH BESSEY[5]

The fact is that these women, most of whom do not appear in the three-year Sunday calendar of readings called the Lectionary, are all figures who suffer from cruel male authority and are the victims of discrimination. Yet they are also agents of God's liberating justice. And there are many more.

In ancient Judaism, women had little authority apart from being child bearers and rearers. Their testimony was not valid in a court of law and the extent to which they suffered discrimination can be found in this piece of legislation:

'When a virgin is pledged in marriage to a man, and another man encounters her in the town and lies with her, bring both of them out to the gate of the town and stone them to death; the girl because, although she was in the town, she did not cry for help, and the man because he violated another man's wife.'
DEUTERONOMY 22:23–24

You can imagine how controversial a ruling that would be today in a rape trial.

This is not to say that the Old Testament is a misogynistic document from start to finish. Not at all. Indeed, the prophecy of Isaiah extols woman's experience from conception to motherhood. And

Jesus, in his ministry, comes not with a negative suspicion about women, but with positive openness.

'Perhaps it is no wonder that the women were first at the Cradle and last at the Cross. They had never known a man like this Man – there never has been such another.'
DOROTHY L. SAYERS[6]

A SURPRISING DISCOVERY

Some years ago in Regina, the capital of the Canadian province of Saskatchewan, I led a biblical reflection which required the company of priests and laypeople to divide into two groups and move to different rooms. I asked one group to name, from memory, all twelve of Jesus' male disciples and identify three things known about each. The other group was to identify twelve of Jesus' female followers and three things known about each. Both groups were to write up their findings on large pieces of card.

When, after fifteen minutes, people came back together, the results were different from what people had anticipated. Of those looking at the disciples, only ten names had been remembered, and when it came to three things about each, well . . . what do we remember about Simon the Zealot, James the Less, Thaddeus, even Matthew?

By contrast, the group looking at Jesus' female followers had plenty to say about Elizabeth, Mary his mother, the sisters Martha and Mary, the woman who washed his feet with her tears, the Syro-Phoenician woman with the sick daughter, the woman who suffered from haemorrhages, and the woman at the well.

Indeed, we discovered that day that there are more verses devoted to the woman at the well than to eleven of the twelve male disciples.[7] She, to some extent, is the first evangelist. She brings a whole village to Jesus; none of the disciples have that accolade.

'Jesus's longest recorded private conversation with anyone in the Gospels is with a woman Jewish men would have avoided at all costs. This woman is the first person in John's Gospel to whom Jesus explicitly reveals himself as the Christ, and she is the last person with whom a respectable rabbi should have been spending time alone.'
REBECCA McLAUGHLIN[8]

In fact, if we read Luke's Gospel, we find out that not only does Luke record eighteen out of the twenty-two women who are close to Jesus, but also that Jesus frequently uses inclusive language contrasting traditionally male and female roles:

- darning a garment and storing wine
- baking bread and sowing corn
- looking for a lost coin and seeking a lost lamb

And when it comes to his death, the only person who actively tried to prevent it was a woman – Pilate's wife.

Jesus does not accord with the demeaning standards of his time regarding the place and potential in women. He engages with them, depends on them, is challenged by them and is trusted by them in a way no other figure in the Bible comes close to equalling. And in the world's religions, it is difficult to find any major leader who engages with and talks to women with such ease.

THE GENTILES

The history of the Jews is one in which the relationship their nation has with surrounding nations is constantly changing. Egypt is a friend during a period of severe famine when Joseph became governor of the country, but a deadly enemy later when a Pharaoh enslaved the Hebrews and initiated a policy of infanticide around the time Moses was born. Occasionally, God seems to be on the side of the Israelites against the foreign foes, as when David slew Goliath; at other moments, God seems to favour the enemies of the Jews, as when Nebuchadnezzar is recorded as being God's agent of justice. Sometimes Jews favour intermingling of nationalities in marriage; sometimes that is regarded as abhorrent.

And then we come to Jesus' genealogy and discover that four of his female ancestors are not Jewish, despite the historical identification of Jewish pedigree as one that is transferred through the mother.

We commonly give the name 'Gentiles' to people living at the time of Jesus who were not Jewish. But this catch-all title is highly misleading. Jerusalem, the capital of Israel, was an international market town – hence the need to have a currency exchange in the Temple. And in the course of Jesus' ministry, he is recorded as engaging with people of at least seven different ethnic groups. Can you identify them? (Try this before continuing to read.)

In chronological order, the first has to be the people known as the wise men who came from Mesopotamia, an area which includes the border regions of what we now call Iraq and Iran. Incidentally, an Irish scholar reckons that the number three (not mentioned in the Bible) and the names given to them (Caspar, Melchior and Balthazar) can be traced back to a sixth-century Irish manuscript.[9]

At any rate, they are the people who first bring gifts to Jesus and affirm his royal status. They also, by going home another way, try to protect him from the effects of King Herod's fear of rivalry.

'Matthew's Gospel demonstrates concern for those removed from the political system by contrasting the disenfranchised with the elite; and by distinguishing those who stay put and remain complacent from those who are displaced and lack permanent homes. "Herod and all Jerusalem" are arrayed against the displaced holy family and the Magi who travel to and from Bethlehem.'
THE WOMEN'S BIBLE COMMENTARY[10]

The second ethnic group are the Egyptians. Egypt – previously enemy territory – is the country to which the Holy Family fled in order to prevent Jesus being killed in the infanticide which Herod unleashed.

The third group are called Greeks, a term which probably signifies foreign identity rather people from that country. These people seek an audience with Jesus and are introduced to him by Philip and Andrew.

Then there are Syrians, two in particular. The first is the Syro-Phoenician woman who argues with Jesus, a conversation which has a double result. The first is what some call an empathy developing in Jesus after she has challenged him for referring to her race as 'dogs'. The second result is the healing of her daughter.

'The story of the Syro-Phoenician makes women's contribution to one of the most crucial traditions in early Christian beginnings historically available. Through such an analysis, the Syro-Phoenician can become visible again as one of the apostolic foremothers of Gentile Christians.' ELISABETH SCHÜSSLER FIORENZA[11]

The second Syrian is not a person Jesus meets, but one he mentions as evidence that God's love (and, implicitly, Jesus' ministry) is not for the Jews alone. This is Naaman, the Syrian commander who is healed of leprosy by the prophet Elisha.[12] For merely citing this, along with another example of a prophet helping a foreigner, the first direct attempt is made on Jesus' life by his fellow countryfolk, who were listening to him preach in his home synagogue.

We have already noted the woman at the well. She is a Samaritan. As well as being a potential candidate for Jesus' first evangelist, she introduces him to people in the community where she lives; and he is so taken by these 'foreigners' that he stays an extra two days in her village.

A leper, whom Jesus heals, is also a Samaritan, and is the only one in a group of ten who returns to give thanks for his healing.[13] In him, Jesus identifies deep gratitude, while noting an absence of gratitude in the other nine men healed of leprosy who were his fellow countryfolk.

Simon of Cyrene is one of possibly two other people who come from Africa. He hailed from the country we now call Libya, and he was the man who helped to carry Jesus' cross to Calvary.

FINALLY, THE ROMANS

And then we have the Romans – of whom three are worthy of mention as people who had a positive attraction to Jesus. One was the unnamed wife of Pharaoh. The second and third were centurions, of whom one had a servant whom Jesus healed, and the other gave Jesus his title after he had died: 'Truly this was the Son of God' (Matthew 27:54).

It would be wrong to presume that these people were Italian just by dint of them being Romans. The Roman army drew people from all over Europe, particularly the lands bordering on the Mediterranean. If a man, living in countries occupied by the Romans, served three years in the Roman army, was exceptionally dutiful and professed loyalty to the Emperor, he could be made a centurion.

There were Roman soldiers of colour in Scotland in the fourth century, so when we read of the Roman centurions in the Gospels, they could have been white, black or brown. They could have come from Turkey, Brittany, Portugal or Morocco. And it is about one of them, whose servant Jesus healed, that he said he had never seen such faith in all Israel.[14]

It was from foreigners that Jesus received gifts – physical tokens from the wise men, but examples of faith, gratitude and generosity of spirit from the others, which consistently contrasted with the suspicion and opposition that came from his fellow Jews, particularly the religious authorities in his own nation.

'I want to be outside with the misfits, with the rebels, the dreamers, second-chance givers, the radical grace lavishers, the ones with arms wide open, the courageously vulnerable, and among even – or maybe especially – the ones rejected by the Table as not worthy enough or right enough.'
SARAH BESSEY[15]

It is interesting to note that on no occasion does Jesus, when involved with people whose ethnicity was other than Jewish, demand of them either conversion or discipleship.

FOR DISCUSSION

1. What, in the foregoing text, has surprised you most and why?

2. Why have the churches been reticent to celebrate the witness of biblical women as much as that of biblical men?

3. What does the refusal of Jesus to ask 'foreigners' to be converted or follow him say to our engagement with people of different faiths?

SESSION 4
A LIFE OF RISK

THE ABSENCE OF INCARNATION

In January 2021, a work entitled 'Christmas Oratorio' by the Scottish composer Sir James MacMillan was given its first performance in Amsterdam. It is a stunning and accessible work for orchestra, choir and two soloists, and has subsequently been performed in England and Scotland to great acclaim.

'Rhythm and harmony find their way into the inmost soul.'
PLATO[1]

'Music expresses that which cannot be said, and on which it is impossible to be silent.'
VICTOR HUGO[2]

Among many noteworthy features is the libretto or text which makes amazingly little reference to the nativity in Bethlehem, but rather moves quickly to the visitation of the wise men, the Slaughter of the Innocents, and the centrality in John's Gospel of the Word becoming flesh.

There is no reason given for what some might see as a glaring omission. But it might have pleased the late John Wilson, who was the foremost British expert on hymn tunes. On one occasion, when I asked him if he was looking forward to Christmas, he grimaced and then responded:

'Oh Christmas! On Christmas Day what I long to do is stay in bed and just think about the Incarnation.'
JOHN WILSON[3]

There is something alluring about the domestic blessing and disarray which is central to the nativity narratives. But, as we explored in an earlier session, the gift of God coming among us in Christ is not primarily that our hearts might be warmed by his humble origins and our consciences laden with guilt because of his crucifixion. There is a life between the cradle and the cross.

'Jesus promised His disciples three things – that they would be completely fearless, absurdly happy and in constant trouble.'
WILLIAM BARCLAY[4]

There are many conjectures regarding why – in the hymnody, the iconography and the liturgy of the Church – so much attention is paid to the extremes. Among them is the interesting suggestion that, because Paul writes little about the life of Jesus, its importance is diminished.

This might seem at first quite outrageous until we ponder these facts:

THE GOSPELS AND THE LETTERS

Matthew's Gospel is the great teaching Gospel, with long passages regarding the will and purpose of God. Paul rarely, if ever, alludes to Jesus' teaching.

Mark's Gospel has a host of miracle stories both to do with healing and intervention in the natural order. Paul never mentions any of these.

Luke's Gospel has the majority of the great parables – the Prodigal Son, the Good Samaritan, The Great Feast. Luke also puts a high profile on women with whom Jesus engages. Paul never alludes to these.

John's Gospel is the latest written of the four, but is replete with titles given to Jesus and has three very substantial stories – the Woman at the Well, the Man Born Blind and the Raising of Lazarus. These don't feature at all in Paul's letters.

Why is this? It must partly be that, as distinct from the moment of his conversion, Paul never met Jesus, and given that the Gospels were not in manuscript form during his life, he could not personally witness to more than his conviction that Jesus died and rose again. He would also be aware that all the apostles apart from Judas Iscariot were still alive, and that the Gospel writers had direct access to some of them, so why should he presume to compete?

And then there is his clear sense of vocation. He is an apologist to the Jews, keen to enable them to come to a belief in Jesus as the Messiah. He is an evangelist to the Gentiles, committed to dismantling any suspicion that Christianity was for the Jews only. And he was a church planter, who had to keep connection with a variety of very different fledgling congregations in different parts of Europe and Asia Minor, who had no blueprint for liturgy, management or community life.

'Saul of Tarsus, in other words, had found a new vocation. It would demand all the energy, all the zeal, that he had devoted to his former way of life. He was now to be a herald of the king.'
N. T. WRIGHT[5]

We cannot blame Paul for saying little about the life of Jesus – but we can note short allusions to his life in what might be two of the oldest hymns of the Church, found in Philippians 2:6–11 and Colossians 1:16–20.

GOSPEL REACTIONS TO JESUS

If we only concentrate on Jesus' birth and death, we may have the impression that the threats to his life by Herod and Pilate were his only experiences of persecution. This is a distorted view, for in the intervening years, all was not 'gentle, meek and mild'. Think, for example, of the consequences for him, in his first sermon in his home synagogue in Nazareth, when he dared to suggest that God loved more than the Jews.

'These words roused the congregation to fury; they leapt up, drove him out of the town, and took him to the brow of the hill on which the town was built, meaning to hurl him over the edge.'
LUKE 4:28–29

Jesus accused the scribes and Pharisees of being – among other things – blind guides, whited sepulchres, twice as fit for hell as those they condemned, hypocrites, full of lawlessness and hypocrisy, snakes and exhibitionists (Matthew 23:1–33).

Were such words said in a calm voice, with no desire to upset or cause any adverse reaction?

After the healing of the man born blind, Jesus suggests to the man's accusers (who earnestly believe that his disability was the result of sin) that they who claim to see are actually infected by blindness. Does he expect them to make no retaliation (John 8:39–40)?

In one wealthy household, Jesus has his feet washed with the tears of a call-girl. When his host upbraids him for allowing this unseemly behaviour, Jesus rails on him and says that, in contrast to the girl who showed an excess of loving care, his host has demonstrated a total lack of kindness. Is this not totally irregular and unmannerly behaviour on the part of a guest? Did Jesus expect to get away with it (Luke 7:36–50)?

'As we meet Jesus in the Gospels, we'll encounter a man who welcomes sexually notorious women while standing up to sexually self-righteous men ... who never had a sexual relationship, but who loved women so well that they'd leave everything to follow him.'
REBECCA McLAUGHLIN[6]

Read the Gospels again. Note the reactions to Jesus, not as articulated by the mellifluous and measured tones of a seasoned reader, but with the animation, anger and embittered speech of people who took exception to his ability to name and shame instances of social injustice. Then we might just get a feeling for a bigger Jesus than that which the Creeds express.

'Events and human actions arouse in Jesus joy or sorrow, pleasure or wrath. He is not conceived as judging the world in detachment. He reacts in an intimate and objective manner and thus determines the value of events.'
JOHN V. TAYLOR[7]

Indeed, we might even grasp how the ancient inhabitants of our shores were not solely evangelised through fear of God's judgement. It was as much through their realisation that the Incarnation was an expression of God's loving desire to enter into solidarity with the world he had made and loved by becoming part of its fabric.

'Nature is the direct expression of the divine imagination.'
JOHN O'DONOHUE[8]

A CELTIC PERSPECTIVE

This certainly was the case with the ancient Celts. For they lived a very precarious existence – as would other tribes in fifth-century Britain.

Consider how, in these early centuries, there were no medicines apart from what could be got from plant and sea life. If there was a disease among the cattle or a plague in the crops, the food stock would run low and starvation might ensue. If people travelled by land where there were neither roads nor street lights, every journey could be dangerous. Sea travel was equally perilous in primitive coracles. And all around coastal regions in Britain and Ireland, there was the fear of predatory Vikings from Scandinavian countries, who did not come to kiss the women and shake hands with the men, but to rape, kill and plunder.

For such people, it was beyond their wildest thinking that the God above (in whom they had a primitive belief) would consider coming among them. Life was too risky for a God above and beyond all. But then he came.

So, I finish with a meditation on the Incarnation.

GOD'S GREAT 'WHAT IF'?[9]

God had delivered legislation by the bucketful through Moses and his devotees, but then as now, legislation did not guarantee goodness.

Through the poets, especially in the Psalms, God had bared the divine heart, expressing anger, yearning, affection and commitment, but that did not necessarily improve the witness and devotion of the chosen people.

Through the prophets, God delivered judgement, warnings, an analysis of how things were and dreams of how they should be, but again to minimal effect.

And then God thought, what if ...?

What if, rather than stay within the boundlessness of eternity, I constrain myself within the limitations of time and space?

What if, rather than be disembodied and therefore omnipresent, I limit myself to the bodily form and intellectual dexterity of a human being?

What if I emerge on earth, not as the gifted child of a pedigreed family, but to be parented by people who have no status or secure locus?

What if, rather than be educated in the finest academy, I learn about life through thirty years of anonymity?

What if, rather than be inviolable, I make myself vulnerable – to pain, to prejudice, to slander, to disease and to the loss of credibility because of what I say and who I associate with?

What if, rather than choose the best graduates from the foremost rabbinic seminary, I pick for my companions a random sample of tradesmen, civil servants, people with financial acumen, maybe even some with no specific skills and one who might be quite untrustworthy?

What if, rather than repeat safe nostrums from the inviolability of the pulpit, I tell the as-yet-uncherished truths about life, faith and divine identity with the effect that outraged people may try to stone me?

What if, should all my attempts to save the world by my life and example fail, rather than return to the safety of heaven, I accept the capital punishment which earth reserves for those whose integrity and compassion are too much to bear?

And what if, when I'm dead, I don't stay lying down?

'While the life that Jesus lived was wholly human, that which was incarnate in him was of the essence of God, the very Son of the Father, very God of very God.'
DONALD M. BAILLIE[10]

FOR DISCUSSION

1. Do you or does your church tend to see Jesus through the eyes of Paul, or Paul through the eyes of Jesus?

2. Why, given all the evidence in the Gospels of the irritation Jesus caused by his anger at injustice, do we have the impression that the only time such things were exhibited was in the cleansing of the Temple?

3. Do you find the notion of the Incarnation as God's risk helpful or distracting ... and why?

TRANSCRIPT
INTRODUCTION

JOHN Hello, wherever you are, and welcome to this Advent course, which, as you know, is called *The Life in the Comma*. My name is John Bell. I am an ordained minister of the Church of Scotland and a member of the Iona Community, and at the moment I'm trying to be retired, which is my present state of affairs.

And this is a topic which I've got a fascination for – the whole issue of Advent. And in the course, we'll be looking, not so much at the things that we all know about Christmas and the birth of Jesus, but about some other things which perhaps have never been touched. And this is a conversation that I'm having, not with myself, but with two people who will now introduce themselves and the first is ...

SMITHA So my name is Smitha Prasadam. I'm Bishop of Huddersfield, and I'd rather say that I feel that I'm a child of God and I'm just one beggar telling another beggar where to find food.

JOHN And we have also ...

LAUREN I'm Lauren Windle. I'm an author and a journalist and I focus on faith and recovery and love and all things in that kind of sphere.

JOHN So, we're going to be together for four different aspects of this whole adventure of Advent into Christmas. We're very glad that you've decided to join us, and we look forward to seeing you at the first session.

SESSION 1
ADVENT – A TIME FOR THE KIDS?

JOHN Hello, and welcome to our Advent course, *The Life in the Comma*, and particularly to Session 1, which is called 'Advent – a time for the kids?'

I want to begin by asking a question which is something that I couldn't give much of an answer to, because my background – I come from Scotland, I'm a Presbyterian, a kind of Calvinist I suppose you might say – and we never knew anything about Advent at all in my childhood. In fact, in Scotland, there was a suspicion even of Christmas, such that, until the 50s, Christmas was not a holiday for people. But I'm wondering if my two friends here have a better story. Is Advent something that's been part of your life, your past?

SMITHA So as far as my Advent, I don't think I was even *aware* of Advent until I was about 18. Because the whole time before, particularly my upbringing in India and in my grandmother's house, I look back on it and think that Advent started on December the 22ⁿᵈ, because that then would be the time that the house would go into flurry about getting ready for Christmas. It also happens to be my birthday, and that of my twin. [*John and Lauren laugh.*] But what was *really significant* for us was the sense of getting ready. My grandmother and mother would go out in search of women particularly, who were on the streets, would bring them to the house. They would be given a meal, they would be given a new sari – and that would be our preparation for Christmas because this was for the coming king, and *that* I realised was a sense of the countdown. It was only three days.

JOHN Goodness! And Lauren?

LAUREN Oh, mine is *so rubbish* compared to that! So, I was sort of 90s London growing up, so any kind of touch points I had with Advent were all the sort of commercial kinds. I had an Advent calendar. I was never allowed a chocolate one, which is a bit gutting ... And I had like, you know, one of those ones where you take a tiny book and then you put it on your tree, and the little book's got a bit of the sort of Christmas story and Jesus' birth, you know, in it as well. So, there were ... my parents did their best to keep Jesus at the centre but a lot of the sort of Hallmark and Clinton's card stuff kind of crept in, and that was my understanding of Advent. It was the time I wasn't allowed a chocolate.

JOHN   Oh my dear! I feel as if I've missed out, you know. I could have had a sari or I could have had an Advent calendar, but I was born in Kilmarnock in Scotland.

The other thing about Advent and Christmas particularly is that, particularly for people of a kind of Protestant background, it was one of the few times when a woman emerged called Mary, who, as Protestants presumed, was a Catholic. You know, Jesus was a, well we didn't give him a denomination. Paul was certainly a Protestant, but Mary was a Catholic. And Advent and Christmas have so much to do with women, but I want us to think about Mary particularly. And we know a little about her. She was the mother of Jesus, so I'm wondering if we might just share a thing about our own mothers. Well, I'll go last. Lauren, give us one thing about your mother, you'd remember.

LAUREN   My mum's phenomenal, but she grew up – this is actually quite a sad story – but she grew up with very little money. She's Scottish as well, but she grew up in Durham, and her dad was a gardener. She was at university – she studied biochemistry – and there was an ... like some sort of gas she was working with that she inhaled, accidentally, and realised that it was a toxic gas, and she thought, well, okay, I'm going to die then. So, she went down to the canteen and treated herself to a prawn sandwich 'cause she wouldn't usually spend that much? On lunch. And she ate a prawn sandwich and she didn't die. She was fine.

But I always think of that as like a sort of moment of real tenderness that actually, you know, she didn't get to treat herself very often. And actually she's *incredibly* generous now, where she's in a bit of a better position to sort of share things with people because she knows what it's like to have so little.

JOHN   Oh.

SMITHA   Mmm.

JOHN   Smitha, what about you, your mum?

SMITHA   My mum, I think Shakespeare wrote some lines, for *her*, four hundred years ago, that she didn't know about: 'Though she be little, she be fierce.' [*John laughs.*] Because she's one of these women who's less than five foot tall. But she can get everywhere and anywhere and she packs a punch wherever she goes. She's noticed, maybe because of her size, maybe because she's a woman in a sari and in a dog collar, and she has been able to do things ... it's a bit like a fairy or an elf really, getting about, working wonders, doing magic, diffusing conflicts, bringing people together, sharing food, having the air of festival about her, and really all with appropriate fun and real godliness. I think that's what I'd say about my mum.

LAUREN   Gosh!

JOHN   Well, my mum's no longer with us, but she kind of sits on my shoulder. She was very keen when we were growing up – we weren't a wealthy family – that we'd eat everything, even things which I didn't like, like tripe or oxtail. And she would compel us, you know, to finish this food. And my father would talk about the starving children in India or in China, who I'd be very glad to have sent the food to, particularly if I didn't want it. But it's meant that, if I'm in company and there's stuff that isn't finished, my mother's on my head ... on my tail ... on my shoulder, I should say, saying, 'Look at all that. That's going to go to waste. That's a scandal.' And so, I eat stuff that I don't need to, because my mother taught me nothing should go to waste.

And we could conjecture for a wee while about, you know, what would Jesus know about his mother and what kind of stories would he tell about his mother? Because we're dealing with a real woman, who brings a child into the world in quite a dilemma, you know. She is not married when she conceives, and there's some suspicion about her, I mean, I've been working with people in Glasgow. We did a nativity play and we talked about, 'What would people in the village say when they saw Mary buying dresses which were a bit too big for her?' I mean, the whole background to this story is one in which there's great risk. But normally, when we celebrate Christmas, people see it through the eyes of children in nativity plays.

Now was that something that you were part of as a child, a nativity play? Would you like to say what you did? Lauren, you're looking not too happy with that.

LAUREN   Star number four, I believe, was my heady heights that I got to on stage in my primary school. I was never Mary. I was never even the biggest star or El Gabriel, you know, despite pushing, year on year, for a better role. So, erm, yeah, I feel a bit tense about it, if I'm honest. [*Everyone laughs.*] I was always in the chorus, twinkling or doing whatever I was sort of told and probably making a mess of it, and just waving at my mum.

JOHN   Aww, aww!

SMITHA   And, unlike Lauren, I was *never* in a nativity play – not as a star, not even as the back end of the donkey! [*John and Lauren laugh.*] I really wasn't! But because of that, I think I went overboard and I tried to make a difference. And especially when I got to parish and I was in Birmingham, we would do, not so much nativity plays, but nativity *journeys* involving the whole community ... the local funeral director would lend me three limousines ...

LAUREN   Wow!

SMITHA   ... out of which would step three kings, the magi, with their wonderful gifts. And out of bus shelters, and so on, would jump out some shepherds on a hillside. And we were in a parish which had a lot of hills, so they were, you know, right out of the hillside, as the children walked to the church, expecting a conventional nativity play. They became the characters. So, the boys and girls would have to take part in the census, and their fingerprints on the papers, and so on, to make it real.

But the way that it came alive for me, the beauty of it, and in the sense of children entering at a different level ... the Christmas story, not the tinsel and twinkling stars, but at a much deeper level, when they encountered Mary and Joseph and this child. We had a makeshift manger with straw and so on, and when different characters were telling the story, I *vividly* remember a child *running*, literally *running* from the back to the front saying, 'You can't have a baby in there! You just can't have a baby in there! It'll die!' And then went on to say the most *amazing* words which are etched in my memory: 'My mother works at the university. There are *so many* rooms in the university. *Please* can we take the baby now to the university?'

JOHN But isn't that such a good recognition of the *risk* of the whole nativity?

Now, we didn't have nativity plays when I was a boy. And I think the nearest I got was singing the third wise man and 'We Three Kings' and I hated it, I hated it. But, for a number of years, two years, I worked in a parish in Glasgow where there was no one who was a professional. Everyone had left school when they were 15. It was a very impoverished area. And I decided that when I worked there – now, I went with a colleague of mine; we would do an evening a week with a group who were trying to develop leadership skills. And we did this every six weeks; we would take another one of the services, evening or morning.

I remember when we did the morning services, and it was coming up to Christmas and they always had a nativity play with children. And I said to these people – there were about maybe ten of them – why don't we do a nativity play with adults? And so, these people who'd never spoken in church before wrote this play from the perspective of adults. It was a *stunning* thing. And they stood, you know they're not people who would stand in the front of an audience, but if they stood round the walls of the church – and it was small enough for everyone to hear – they would speak from there. And they spoke in the vernacular, and, you know, Mary was misshapen; she wasn't eternally slim. An old man, a retired taxi driver who was an alcoholic called John, was an angel. And I remember when he said, when the narrator said, 'So God sent to Mary the angel Gabriel', and this 76-year-old recovering alcoholic said, 'I am that angel.' And all the kids who are sitting in the middle of the church were like ... Well, why could that not be an angel? They had never seen an angel before, and it could be somebody who looked quite unusual.

Right at the end, which links in with your story, we had this ... three orange boxes, and we had a wee carol called Cloth for the cradle, and teenagers came and put the orange boxes, two upright, one across, and then everyone in the congregation had a strip of cloth. And as we sang, people could come out and lay the cloth over the orange box to make it the kind of manger in which you could safely put a baby.

Now this was symbolic action, which Protestants are not good at. And it was the most moving thing to see ... You know, a girl taking her cloth and putting it over the manger, and then going back and taking her grandmother by the hand and bringing her up. And it was the same kind of thing as you were saying that ... this now became a reality. This is a story which is about risk. It's a story which is a lot about women. It's a story which has perhaps been over-sanitised, and the crudeness of it ...

SMITHA   Sanitise is the absolute word. Sanitise. We sanitise it, we domesticate it, we try to contain it. Because the message is so big, so wonderful, so not just for us. I think that habit of selfishness, of trying to keep it for us, keep it tidy, keep it safe ... it's God in a box actually, but it's not: it's God for the world.

LAUREN   I think the way that we ... I understand needing to adapt the stories for a child audience, because they're not gonna understand some of those risks around childbirth, and maybe we don't wanna go into the graphics of physical pain Jesus may have felt, and things like that. But, we can sometimes package these incredible life-changing stories in the same way that we do any fairy story, or any sort of tale that sounds a bit unusual, or that's interesting, or has a bit of a moral that we tell children when they're young.

And I know that growing up ... so I stopped engaging with faith at around the age of 13. When I came back at 25, I still thought the Bible was just a collection of fairy stories. Guy's hair's cut, he loses his strength. Giant boat for the flood, you know, all of this stuff. It was actually when I sat and read the Gospels, that you realise the relevance and the reality of it. And that, I think is something I'm still unpicking, still uncovering from the sort of stories I was so familiar with as a child ... Kind of erasing that ... oh yes, that story ... and reassessing it and going, okay, what does that actually mean? It's not just being Mary's carrying a child, like socially, in society, that is *such a risk*! She has *no idea* what the reception will be from people around her; how Joseph's going to react. It's not just the case of, Okay I'll do that quick job, like ... that is just the most *phenomenal* leap of faith, the biggest amount of courage to say, right okay. Oh yes, I'll do this thing, God, you know ...

SMITHA   And to cope with the stigma ...

LAUREN   Yeah!

SMITHA   ... to cope with the kind of unknown in terms of childbirth when many died – both mother and the child ...

JOHN   Oh, oh, I think at the time it was one in three children died at the moment of birth, or before it, and one in four women died in childbirth. This is a great time for us to stop.

LAUREN   I feel like we're just getting started.

JOHN   I know we're just getting started, and we're going to go further. And one of the things which I suppose we realise, is that the phrase, 'Christmas is a time for the kids', is a misnomer. It's a time when God asks adults to do quite extraordinary things.

Thanks very much for being with us. We've enjoyed this session together. We hope you have. And we look forward to being with you for 'The life omitted', which is Session 2.

SESSION 2
THE LIFE OMITTED

JOHN   Hello again, and welcome to our Advent series and to the second session which is called 'The life omitted'.

One of the fascinations which happens in Advent is the whole image of the mother and child. It seems to me to be an iconic image all through the world. And ... I remember being in Vietnam and seeing an image of the mother and child which really took me by total surprise. It wasn't, you know, Mary and Jesus, but it was this mother who was lying flat on the floor, and the child was suckling at her breast. So you could put this any way up, but really it was like looking from the top to the bottom, and seeing a mother lying there and a child suckling at her breast. And the intimacy of that suddenly, you know, struck me in a way I'd never seen before.

And I wonder whether sometimes the icons that we have of Mary and Jesus don't exactly look as if they're very normal. Would that be your experience?

SMITHA   Absolutely. It's Mary looking holy and wholly untouchable, and you could not imagine her, even though we sing it, with a breast full of milk. Because, you know, you can't talk breast and milk and feeding of a child, you know, because she looks too statuesque, to coin a phrase, for that. But the real mother, scooping up the child in her arms, throwing the child up almost in play, singing to her child, *that's* the kind of image that I want to see of Mary! And I've really had to go looking for those. And there are some beautiful images in Indian art, telling that kind of *fuller* motherhood, *fuller childhood* of Jesus.

And if you look at the artwork of people like Jyoti Sahi or Solomon Raj, they are wonderful. And I've had to re-educate myself.

JOHN   Have you anything in your mind about mother and child ...?

LAUREN   It was really fascinating when I read what you said about people being up in arms seeing Mary pregnant.

And you think, like, well where was she supposed to put it? [*Everyone laughs.*] Like, it's crazy that we ... *of course*, Mary is to be revered and respected and honoured for the sacrifices that she made. But, we've divorced her sacrifice from the reality of motherhood, from the way her body would have changed, from actually, the way caring for a child is messy and chaotic, and it's not the sort of pure clean sort of images that we see all the time.

JOHN   Sure.

LAUREN You know, God made it that way. I think in society in general we can sort of expect mothers to tuck away, and parents, to tuck away the difficulty of childbirth and things, but *nowhere* more so than when we're talking about Mary and the birth of Jesus.

JOHN   Now, this is the dominant image which you get until you come to the crucifixion. And it's interesting that when, you know, you ask people what Jesus was like as a person, you have these words 'gentle, meek and mild'. And I wonder why is it that ... I'm trying to think of much Christian art which actually has, at least from a European perspective, a notion of Jesus actually growing up, being engaged with people, laughing with people, eating with people, arguing with people. These kind of depictions seem to be gloriously absent, both from the world of art, and also from the world of hymns. You know, very few hymns actually speak about the life of Jesus. And I wondered, you know, whether we have to, kind of, do something different than just keep this domestic holy person, who never gets angry or is difficult or is awkward ... erase that from our minds? What do you think?

LAUREN I definitely, I *definitely* grew up seeing Jesus as not massively relevant. Because what I saw of him was so unobtainable. And, you know, it's a guy floating around, you know, in his ... in his ...

SMITHA [*Laughs.*] Long robes ...

LAUREN ... sparkling robes, you know, just imparting wisdom in complex stories and then floating away again. And actually, particularly growing up, I didn't really enjoy being in church because it was Christians who sort of put forward that judgemental, that holier-than-thou, that always right kind of attitude and depicted that for me when it comes to Jesus. But when you look at it, my goodness, you know, yes, there was the gentleness that we speak about, but it was, sort of, cloaked in absolute power. Jesus doesn't get sort of knocked down and have a little whimper on the floor; he dusts his knuckles off, he gets back up, he, you know, brushes the blood off his face and goes again. And *that's* the kind of Saviour ...

SMITHA   The *real* Jesus ...

LAUREN   Yeah!

SMITHA   The real Jesus ... the full-bodied ...

JOHN   The full-bodied ... [*He and Lauren laugh.*]

SMITHA   No! *Full-bodied* – he makes it sound like a wine! [*Everyone laughs.*] He poured his blood ... But *the full-bodied, charismatic, magnetic* Jesus, the one who you look at and go, '*Phwarr!*'

LAUREN   Yeah.

SMITHA   You know, it's that kind of real Jesus. He *must* have had something about him which drew the crowds. And I'd like that to be seen. I mean, I don't want to go and see somebody who doesn't look as if he could say boo to a goose because he's looking so gentle and mild.

JOHN   But I'm wondering whether you think there might have been a conspiracy ... to avoid that?

SMITHA   I'm sure there is, because that kind of Jesus is problematic. That kind of Jesus is a rabble rouser. That kind of Jesus is a revolutionary, who fulfils his mother's song. He turns the values of the world upside down. And he asks us to rethink *everything* that we think of as cultural norms, or things that we accept because this is what society is like. But he asks us to look again, look again through, not only the compassion of God, but the justice and care and the love of God, and say, okay, go and do something about this. So, *this* kind of Jesus for me ...

JOHN   Yeah, there's something about the passivity which has got me. Now I remember being in a Bible study in ...

somewhere in Australia. It was men only and we were looking at the story of the raising of Lazarus. And I remember this man, who was a professor of dental medicine, being quite perturbed when I read the story to this group of people, so that they could get used to my accent and also so that the way we read it was one in which there was time to just take in the different periods in this long story in John's Gospel. And this guy was really fixated about how the translation I was using said that, when Jesus saw Mary weeping, and the people with her weeping, he was indignant. And he said to us, what does indignant mean? I thought, 'You're a learned man; you're a professor.' I says, 'Well, it means he was angry, in fact he was very angry.' 'No,' he said, 'that's not possible.' I said, 'What do you mean?' He says, well . . . He says, 'I've never known Jesus Christ to be angry.' And I was thinking, no, this is personal testimony!

LAUREN Tell that to the tables in the temple! [*Everyone laughs.*]

JOHN Well, quite! But then you look at the Gospels and you find that anger is part of his emotional vocabulary. And I asked this man, 'What is it that has made you think he could never be angry?' And then he quoted a hymn about how 'no one marked an angry word who ever heard him speak'. And this is totally errant. The song has depicted a Jesus who is deficient. He has a limited emotional vocabulary. Now, I'm wondering whether, in the world of culture or arts or music or song or whatever, you've ever felt, here is an alternative which is worth hanging on to?

LAUREN Gosh, you know the picture books, the kids' stuff I engaged with when I was younger in the 90s tended to be that classic picture of floating, white Jesus, white robes, you know, all of that kind of stuff. And I definitely think that it affected the way I felt comfortable interacting with this Jesus person as I was trying to sort of build that personal relationship.

I think, I wouldn't say that I have adopted this as my sort of mental image of Jesus, but I read *The Shack*, and then, watching the film of it, where God is a sort of matronly black woman, and Jesus is sort of an actual man who was from the region and, you know, and then you've got this quite sort of floaty holy spirit. But what it did do, is encourage me to look wider than the small picture I had in my head. And if I have said this is what Jesus is like, this is what God looks like, I'm making it too small.

So, that actually I found, even though there was a bit of controversy around it at the time, I actually found really helpful because if we're saying, this is what Jesus looked like, this is how he was, and we're sort of taking things from hymns and from pop culture and from kids' books that show him the sort of floaty, ethereal person, then that's wrong, you know. But the best source of re-evaluating that is definitely the Bible. When you *really* look at it and understand the gravity of those situations.

JOHN I mean, for me, one of the times was going to *Godspell* – before you were conceived! – and seeing David Essex using the words in Luke's Gospel and bringing them totally alive in a way I had never, ever imagined, that the humour that was there, that the anger that was there, that the sarcasm, all had been devolved from my understanding. It changed my image of Jesus for ever.

SMITHA And for me the overarching image is *Jesus Christ Superstar*, which I saw on stage, and then I saw the film also around about the same time. And it was amazing! And I can tell you in that theatre in Cardiff, which is where I saw it, as the lashes were struck on Jesus, the stage lit up with each lash. There was another segment of the stage that lit up, and the horror, the agony, all of that, was fully there, fully present.

However, when I think of something in art which made a *huge* impression on me, which was very different, was *Written on the Heart*. And it's a play by David Edgar, and it was to mark the four hundredth anniversary of the King James Bible. And *how much* there had been four hundred years ago about Tyndale and Lancelot Andrewes, bringing the Bible into the vernacular, so that Jesus was understood. Jesus was that bit *nearer*. It was easy for us to understand the words that he spoke, rather than some archaic language.

LAUREN   Sometimes when I speak for non-Christian audiences, I will opt for *The Message* interpretation rather than a more traditional translation. And I do say, I really encourage you to read this in a translation, in NIV or whatever as well, just because it's language that's so much easier to connect with. And people are shocked that you can hear Jesus' words in that language rather than the thous and th'arts.

JOHN   That word shocked is very apposite. There's a ... it's mentioned in the booklet that in Glasgow there's this image of *The Christ of St John of the Cross.*

LAUREN   Yeah!

JOHN   And, I've found that a transforming ... it's only recently that I realised that, partly because I was brought up to think that's a Catholic image and what's it doing in our art gallery, all that kind of nonsense ... And then you look at it, and you see that this is the crucifixion of the most beautiful being in the world; that in Christ the fullness of God dwelt. And it wasn't a wretch who was being crucified; it was something which was immensely, immensely, more imaginably greater than our best idea of what a human being could be, and yet it was incarnate in Jesus.

It made me wonder whether, in the depictions of Jesus, or in the conversation about Jesus, or the songs about Jesus, we kind of miss that kind of glorious bigness of God, that fullness of God, and that sometimes the joy which Jesus says, 'I've come that my joy may be in you and make your joy complete', it's substituted for guilt! In our liturgies and in our songs, there's an overriding concentration on the guilt that we should feel because Jesus died, rather than the joy that we should experience because Jesus lives.

LAUREN   Yeah.

SMITHA   And that sense of joy is what I think we need to relearn. Effervescence, which is there, you know, the joy that bubbles out because Jesus in you makes such a difference to your life, and to the life of others. The image that you talk about, isn't it beautiful? That perspective that you see, and the really broad shoulders – and you use the word unblemished – and it really brings it home that this is the cosmic Christ, not the one who came to Christians in church, but to the world. And please let's also not forget, to people of other faiths, who recognise Jesus as somebody special, good and holy, and yet we try and claim him for ourselves. But it's much bigger.

LAUREN   I spend so much time trying to encourage people not to see Jesus as the fun police. Who you just go to, yeah, with guilt. It's actually like, oh, got that wrong again, got that wrong again. Like actually, as you said earlier, people were drawn to him; he turned things on their head; he provided answers and warmth and stability, to people who felt that they didn't have any of that. It's exciting to see what can happen through Jesus. It's not just a list of things you can't do any more that you sort of quite enjoy. It's actually like the fullness, the newness, everything he can do because of that monumental sacrifice.

JOHN   And you know when you read the Gospels, you find that when he speaks about guilt or sin, it's more what he perceives in the lives of those who think they're most holy.

LAUREN   Oh yeah.

JOHN   And when he comes to cure people – this is very interesting, I found this recently – when he comes to heal people, there's only one of the healing miracles in which confession of sin is mentioned. He doesn't ask questions. This person has to have the fullness of God in them, and at this moment, that will happen.

Well, it's time to close, sadly. But we're very glad that we've had this conversation, and we hope that you will have great conversations, and that you'll be with us for the next episode, which is called 'Unspoken in Advent'.

SESSION 3
UNSPOKEN IN ADVENT

JOHN   Hello again. We're back to speak about 'Unspoken in Advent'. Now this might seem a kind of curious title for this session, but I want to begin with exploring something which is really unspoken in Advent. And that's namely that, when you look in Matthew's Gospel and you see the genealogy and the people, the ancestors of Jesus, you find that among them there are four women.

Now, all the men who are there presumably had wives. But, there are only four women mentioned and, I'm wondering, given that there are two women here, whether you have any idea why these four should have been picked and not the others. Not even Abraham's wife, Sarah – she doesn't get a mention – but Ruth and Bathsheba and the two others ...

SMITHA   Basically, a prostitute and an outsider, a foreigner – these are the people who get mentioned. And I find that *incredible*. I have to say that, in the past, when the Matthew genealogy was read out in church, A begat B begat C begat D. And I would listen out for the times that begat was spoken aloud, instead of listening for who.

So, I think in my childhood, I missed out those four amazing women, who were so significant to salvation history. Because they are the unlikely women. But they're the women who are named. And these, unlike other women who are written about in the Gospels – and it always seems to me that women when they're mentioned in the Bible are barren or bent double or weeping [*John and Lauren laugh*], you know – but my gosh, are these *feisty* women, *fearless* women, *faithful* women, yet *foreign* women!

And yet they're at the *core* of Jesus' story, and therefore ours. And so now I sit up. I don't listen to the begats. I listen to the women, and I go, 'Woooo!' When the women are mentioned! [*John and Lauren laugh.*]

LAUREN   They're unlikely heroes, aren't they? They're people who would have been dismissed, who *were* dismissed, we *see* them dismissed. They're widows, they're prostitutes, rape victims, and they're *there*, and it's acknowledging that their decisions, their faith, that led them to have children in the way that they did, changed the course of history, and fed into Jesus. And that is, considering that was documented at a time when the sort of Greco-Roman society of the day just did not value women. It was all about your patriarchal lineage. You would only recognise the men. Women, when they were born, were ... often the first daughter was just given the dad's name. And then after that they were numbered. So, you didn't even bother, you know, that was it. They were part of the sort of society, part of trading ... they were a tool, you know. Whereas here, Jesus is going like, no, this ...

SMITHA   *Matters ...*

LAUREN   ... this *matters*, and that's just so amazing.

JOHN   Now, I had this very unusual experience of being in a church in the Midlands one Sunday when this was being read. And it was read in a particular way, the genealogy of Jesus, in that the priest – it was an Anglican church – read until it came to a woman's name. And then a woman in the congregation would stand up and say, 'Let me tell you about Bathsheba.'

SMITHA   Oh, wow!

JOHN   Or: 'Let me tell you about Ruth.'

LAUREN   Wow!

JOHN   And told the story of these women, as if they're talking about their neighbour or their sister or their cousin, very, very clearly. So, after the service, you know, people are invited to go for coffee and I went for coffee, and I'm standing next to this woman, who would be maybe about 24, 25, but you could tell in her face that she's a woman who'd gone through hard times. I just got talking. I said, 'Are you regularly at this church?' She said, 'Yes.' I said, 'Well, I'm not, I've just come in today. It's the nearest church to where I was staying last night.' So, we talk a bit, and then I said, 'Did you enjoy the service this morning?'

'Oh yes,' she said. 'And I loved, you know, Jesus' family tree being read.' I said, 'What, all these old men's names?' She said, 'No, no, the bits when the women told the story ... of these four female characters.' I said, 'This looks quite important to you.' She said, 'It is.' She said, 'You see, I used to be a prostitute, and I became pregnant, and I gave up being a prostitute, and I began to be associated with a community of faith, and I came to believe in Jesus.

'And I have a son who, at the moment, is 5 years of age. And, the time will come, when I want myself to tell him what I once was, before he hears it from anyone else. And on *that* day, I'll be able to say that there is a place in the family tree of Jesus for people like me.'

I mean, wasn't that just such an astounding thing?

SMITHA AND LAUREN   That's so amazing, so amazing!

JOHN   I know, and if these four women were just in that story, so that this one woman could come to faith ...

SMITHA   Amazing. Amazing. It's a bit like that in Ruth, isn't it? Four short chapters, telling the story of Ruth and what a journey, really. And then she's called a foreigner, is it, about fifteen times in four chapters! Outcast, outsider, foreigner, you know, not one of us, is the message all the time. But, the way that Jesus' ministry was, or the one we should be telling, is where the prostitute has an honoured place at his table, where the outsider is an alongsider with him. It's beautiful.

JOHN   And it's interesting when you think of the Advent stories going up to Christmas, that the main players are women or outsiders. You know, there's only one kind of establishment figure, really, and that's the husband of Elizabeth.

SMITHA   Yes.

JOHN   Who's a priest. Zachariah. But you've got big part played by Elizabeth and big part played by Mary. And then later on, you have Anna who's the prophet or the prophetess in the temple. And the wise men are outsiders. They are different, you know, from different race. And shepherds weren't exactly incorporated to mainstream society.

SMITHA   Yeah.

JOHN   Among other things, they didn't have a Sabbath off because sheep didn't decide [*Smitha laughs*] you'll be still for a day. And so, the story, there's much of it about women and about outsiders. And the women involved ... one's very old, you know, Anna. And so is Elizabeth. She's very old. And then Mary is, we don't know her precise age, but she's not ... there's an irregularity about her conception. So, it's a fascinating story. But it dawns me that women in the life of Jesus are really very significant, you know, there are these three right at the beginning. And yet, for some reason, it's mostly *the men* ...

SMITHA   I'm laughing because I'm just thinking, why is it women are not included? It isn't just about two thousand years ago. It is happening right now, because this is the year that we're celebrating women's priest ... ordination to priesthood is the thirtieth anniversary; as bishops, it's the tenth anniversary.

LAUREN   Mm.

SMITHA   This is nascent stuff within the life of the Church. Why have we been so scared of it? And I sometimes think it's because women have been seen to do the domestic roles of feeding, sheltering, caring, being there in terms of the healing ministry, burying the dead. If they can do all that, *and lead as well*, that topples structures and the status quo. I think that's why we have been so scared of women being mentioned, women being praised, women being included, and women leading ... the telling ...

JOHN   [*Laughs.*] I remember – this is a wee bit kind of name dropping – but years ago I was asked to preach in Westminster Abbey Evensong.

LAUREN   Oooh! I'm still waiting for my invite. [*John and Smitha laugh.*]

SMITHA   And me!

JOHN   Now, I can't remember exact detail, but I looked at what they were reading from the Old Testament in the morning. And the Old Testament was the Israelites to God because of the cruelty of the Egyptians.

And then the evening reading, for Evensong, was God's call to Moses. And I thought, there's something missing in between. So, there's about forty verses of the Bible not being read! And they were a good old Anglican church! And then you read it and you discover it's all about women.

It's about Shiphrah and Puah. It's about Moses' mother. It's about Moses' sister, and about Pharaoh's daughter. And had these women not conspired together to bring Moses into life and keep him safe, there would have been no exodus.

LAUREN Yeah.

JOHN And I was thinking, why has this been omitted?

LAUREN Yeah.

JOHN So, when I began to preach Evensong, I said, 'Now friends, I just want to say something, which is that between Morning Prayer and Evensong, it seems that five Middle Eastern women have gone missing.' [*Everyone laughs.*]

SMITHA Lovely!

LAUREN Oh, my goodness!

JOHN There's an old canon there, I thought he was going to die.

LAUREN I liked you before ...

JOHN No, no, no!

LAUREN ... but I really like you now. [*John and Smitha laugh.*]

JOHN But you think, is it because women are not named as much as men? I mean, we've got the twelve disciples, but there are a whole lot of women who are not named.

LAUREN Well, it's interesting. You know, that's such an interesting example to bring up before asking that question because the person who wasn't named in the Moses story is the King, is the Pharaoh, but we know Shiphrah and Puah. We know who they were. The two midwives who just made a decision to ignore a rule from their ruler. They're the ones who got to go down in history. They're the ones who we still remember and celebrate, hopefully, unless you're, you know, in between [*John and Lauren laugh*], but even so! But yes, they aren't, they aren't ... In the Jesus story, there are loads of, loads of women. And I loved reading ... like the sort of statistics that you pull together about how many are there and how we know the characteristics of them. We know more of their character. We know more about their lives than often the men who *are* named. I think it is so clear that women were, were horrifically sidelined, and it's so affirming when you see that society says, 'Don't educate women', and Jesus says, 'No, she's chosen what's good. Leave her here with me.'

You know, we've got blokes now who would *never* let a woman pay for them on a date. But Jesus was very happy to have his ministry, you know, funded by women! [*Everyone laughs.*] He's not lost his masculinity, has he? No! Like, we can look to him. We can see *the way* that he treated these women. And every single time, we see him afford them *more dignity* than the day said to. And that, oh, my goodness! You know, we can't believe the testimony of women. But yet, *they* were the people who got to testify to the ...

SMITHA   Who were around him.

LAUREN   Yeah.

JOHN   But you have to ask, why is it that it's taken us until this time in history, not just to do with the ordination of women, but it's taken us almost this time in history to realise the significance of women to Jesus and he as a liberator of women from the stigma which surrounded them.

LAUREN   Yeah.

JOHN   I mean, sometimes I lie awake at night thinking, why has it taken so long?

LAUREN   Yeah. Jesus gave women a voice, and at some point, Church and religion took it back. And we can see that the tide is changing, you know, celebrating thirty years of women in ordination. But there's still a lot more work to do. And I think that we just need to keep coming back to the way Jesus treated those women. The, you know, what would Jesus do? What a cliché, but there we go, you know. The way that he elevated them; that he didn't punish them more severely than a man. You know, the, the adulterous woman ... that he didn't say, get away from me because you've been ostracised; woman at the well, or the, or the woman who was bleeding, you know, he ...

SMITHA   The fullest stories are actually with Jesus and women.

LAUREN   Yeah! [*John laughs.*]

JOHN   They are!

LAUREN   He was just reeling them off, left, right and centre!

SMITHA   It's wonderful! It's absolutely wonderful. And I know we're talking at the time of Advent, but when you think about the cross, who are the ones who didn't desert, run away, deny ... these were the women who stood facing the horror at the cross. But also were the first at the tomb! [*Everyone laughs.*] And then first to spread the joyous message. So, I think women are integral.

JOHN   Now, the other thing is that, in the Advent and Christmas stories, we have, we have foreigners coming in, you know, we have the wise men who come in and who recognise, *they* recognise ... And it's interesting that, in Jesus' ministry, he sometimes sees in the foreigner the virtue he doesn't see in his own people. You know, when he, he heals the centurion's servant or son ... and the centurion says ...

SMITHA   Or the ten lepers ...

JOHN   Yeah, 'I've never seen faith in all Israel apart from, apart from this.' So, what does that say to us who live as we all do in a multicultural society, when Jesus seems to be as accepting and open to the non-Jew ... as he is to his own people?
Does that have something to say to the way in which we live in a pluralistic society?

SMITHA   There's something I think about the outsider, the foreigner, the stranger being an instrument of God's grace.

LAUREN   Mmm.

SMITHA   I think we see it here in the nativity narratives, but also throughout. You know, and we tend, you know, to identify by race or class or gender or language, 'othering' people in a way.

LAUREN	Yeah.
SMITHA	But I use the term, instrument of grace, instrument of revelation, a different way of seeing. So, I think for us especially, it's to say, 'Let's have the composite story. Let's tell a fuller story. Let's include the stranger. Let's attune our ears in the same way.' And there are people amongst whom we all live, who are unable to tell their story, their fuller story. And so, I think there's a lot about invitation, about welcome, about inclusion, about the kind of participation of people who might be strangers, foreigners, through circumstance, not through their own choice, in many ways. But for whom to be alongside, to be integrated, to be 'one with' is, is something that's so *vital* in our society and in our churches.
LAUREN	I think we need a bit of humility as well to recognise that we're all outsiders. We're all immigrants. We're all foreigners. You know, I've done my genealogy and bit of this, bit of that, bit of Viking, bit of Scottish, bit of ... Someone's moved at some point, haven't they? For me to end up where I am in London and in England.
	So, actually, we're all very different and that's kind of what unites us. So, just because you visibly fit in to the area you are, or you have got a certain accent or a certain language, or, you know, actually everyone ... There, there's so much movement, you know, there's so much moving around.
	We can't 'other' people. It's, you know, Jesus ... We like to think that, if Jesus came knocking on our door, we'd be like, oh yeah, you know, come on in. Or Mary, yes, have my guest room. But how often do we show that kind of welcome to the people around us?
SMITHA	And so discovering, discerning rather than discriminating, I think.
JOHN	See, I kind of get the impression that, in the foreigner and the one who is not, you know, the pedigree Jew, Jesus receives the gifts that he doesn't receive from elsewhere.
	I had this curious thing when, I don't know how long ago it would be ... maybe about twelve years ago, I

went to my doctor's and I said, 'I'd like an appointment with Dr Montgomery', and the, the receptionist said, 'Oh, he's retired.' 'Oh,' I said, 'I thought doctors waited until you died before they retired.' [*Smitha and Lauren laugh.*] 'Oh no,' she said, 'no, he's very healthy, he's very healthy.'

So I said, 'Eh, well, is there another doctor I could see?' And the receptionist said, 'Yeah, we've got two new doctors. In fact, em, there's a cancellation here. And if you want, eh, you could see Dr Ali in twenty minutes.' And I thought, 'Oh, Dr not McAlee, Dr Ali.' So, the first shock was when Dr Ali appeared and said, 'Mr Bell?'

And here is this *beautiful* woman, who is from the Islamic background. And I'd never met a female doctor before. So that, this is a bit of a novelty. And then we go in and we begin to talk. I realised that she's an Iraqi Muslim. But when I was going into her surgery, I thought, 'Has God set this up so that I may convert her?'

And then I thought, 'Well, I think God might have chosen a better time than when I'm trying to get a verruca taken off (*Smitha and Lauren laugh*] my feet.' But I did, for that moment ... and then I thought, 'This is a stupid thing. Jesus never, when he met someone not of his faith, began to ask them what they believed.' And I came to a kind of conclusion. A, that she's the best doctor in the world. She is. I love her dearly. She is ...

LAUREN   That verruca's gone is it? [*Everyone laughs.*]

JOHN   She is. That's right. And, and she is, she's a practising Muslim and she is a *gift* to me and to my health. I began to think, maybe I should pray that Dr Ali should be the best Muslim that she can be, and hope that I can be the best Christian for her ...

SMITHA   Yes.

JOHN   ... that I can be.

SMITHA   And I think that is our conversation with each other, isn't it? That we help each other along the journey of faith. And that we see it through another's eyes. And that helps me to be a better Christian; Dr Ali, to be the better Muslim.

JOHN   This has been a great conversation and we've ended thinking about a life of faith.

Next time we meet, we're going to talk about a life of risk. Please join us then.

SESSION 4
A LIFE OF RISK

JOHN   Hello again, and welcome to the last of our four
        sessions, which is called 'A life of risk'.
        I want to begin, though, with something different,
        because this series has been called *The Life in the
        Comma*, and that came about, partly because it has
        annoyed me for a while, that so much of the Christian
        faith, or at least its expression, seems to be summed
        up in the Creed. And the Creed has, born of the Virgin
        Mary, comma, suffered under Pontius Pilate. It's a big
        fat comma. [*Lauren laughs.*] I mean, that's thirty-three
        years of a life, which is being subsumed. I wondered
        whether *that* has perhaps been a cause of how we've
        missed out on the incarnate life of Jesus, and spent more
        time on his birth and his death than on anything else.

SMITHA It's interesting, isn't it? The only other story between the
        zero and the thirty-three is the boy at twelve ... ish in
        the temple, doing his father's work. But what about the
        boy who had siblings? What was he like at play? At
        conversation? Running about the village? What was he
        like? *Those* are the stories which would inspire me. All
        the bits that are missing.
        And in art – we've talked in a previous session
        about this – where I've only seen one picture, which
        is called *The Smiling Christ*; another, which is *The
        Laughing Christ*; a third, which is *The Angry Christ*.
        And those have made a huge impact on me. Because
        I realise we don't have those stories, and yet this is the
        Christ who was born, and till that moment of death,
        had been an adventurer, a risk taker, who got the
        crowds excited! I would *love* to know those stories!

JOHN   And you know, it strikes me that, if you're being called
        to discipleship, we're not being called by God, either
        to be born of a virgin or to be crucified on a cross.
        Discipleship is about following the life of Jesus, and
        therefore that has to be something which is much more
        evident and celebrated.

LAUREN   And actually, we can see these, like, huge, momentous moments like his birth and his resurrection, and we can forget that the beauty of the mundane, and actually the beauty in the quiet moments, the moments where actually nothing was happening; the times when he was being formed and not even the sort of forty days, you know, actually just day in, day out, the sort of slow formation ... his relationship with his heavenly Father, and how that formed him and gave him that sort of wisdom, you know, to do these incredible, this incredible ministry.

SMITHA   There's something, isn't there, about God is who God is in Jesus. And therefore we have hope. And I think that hope, there is a lot said about hope, but we see that throughout the life of Jesus. The life that's lived in the comma; that he is the one who gives us hope; he is the one who was the ... the one who took the *risk*! You know, who is going to have, eh, great books written about them? Not necessarily ... But our lives are caught up in that life in the comma.

JOHN   Yeah, and this is kind of going off key a wee bit, but I was just thinking – and it's partly going back to a previous conversation – we get children to do nativity plays and there are some children who will maybe kind of re-enact ... Wouldn't it be great if children *played* the *other* scenes in Jesus' life? You know, *played* him in the Pharisee's house, where a woman is washing his feet with her tears. You know, played the engagement of him with the woman at the well. So that this becomes incorporated, not just something which is talked about, but something which is really ingested because we have gone through it.

Now I want to ... in the booklet, there's this quotation by William Barclay, who is a great, eh, Scot, you know? And he [*John and Smitha laugh*] ... and a lovely biblical scholar. And he said, 'Do you often feel as a disciple completely fearless, absurdly happy and in constant trouble?'

SMITHA   Well, I have to say, [*laughs*] thinking about the quote, I'm probably sometimes fearless; often happy; always in trouble! [*Everyone laughs.*] And, uh, you know, I'm a bit like Peter in this regard. I'm sure I say the wrong thing at the wrong time. But I want to be more like Jesus, sometimes asking the challenging questions. Maybe sometimes I am a coward. But, I do want to look in the way that he looks. And yes. Maybe, you know, this thing about being fearless ... I don't know about *completely*, I haven't mastered that skill yet. But, some of our devotion to Jesus, or our discipleship, calls on us, I think, absolutely to that radical path; to fearlessness; to rising to the challenge; to having the brave conversation; to telling that greater story – and asks us to behave, act, be, slightly different.

LAUREN   Yeah.

SMITHA   I don't know what you think?

LAUREN   I think I have pockets of complete fearlessness. Pockets. That only comes when I *know* – you can feel something bubbling in you; God is telling you to do something. And often for me, it starts with me going, 'Oh, very funny. I'm obviously not going to do that.' And then going, 'Okay, I could see how possibly I could do that.' And then going, 'Maybe, maybe I should do that?' And then going, 'Okay, finally, right, God, I'm gonna do that.' And, and that is always the process. I'm always like, 'Oh no thank you. No, I think you probably mean someone else.' And then it slowly dawns on me that God means me. And in *those* moments where I feel so, I feel so sure that I've heard what God is saying and that he's walking with me and that's what he wants me to do, I feel fearless.

And I believe that that fearlessness is accessible to me at all times. And it's me who puts the barrier in place, so that I'm only experiencing in pockets. So, for an example, I'm in recovery from alcohol and drug addiction and have been for coming up to about ten years. And speaking about that for the first time, is something that I initially never thought I would do publicly, but it really felt right in that moment. It's probably the first time I sort of did anything publicly about it. I didn't feel scared, even though it was absolutely terrifying thing to do. And I'd say I've got a funny relationship with happiness. I probably pursue a sort of, you know, wholeness, fulfilledness, that doesn't always feel very happy, but is still ultimately good.

But definitely feel that gratitude, particularly in sobriety. And when it comes to being in constant trouble, that's probably, as you say [*laughs*], the one I relate to the most. And I'm always speaking to churches. No one wants me at their post-church parties because it's about the amount of alcohol they're serving. And, you know, is that really necessary? And I said to my mum, 'I just feel like I'm the church's problem child.' And she said, 'You're the voice of the church. It's problem children ... just really nice!' So, I relate to, to definitely to parts.

JOHN   I remember when I'd finished the job that I was doing in youth work, I had to go to the presbytery, which is the equivalent of a diocese in the Presbyterian Church. And somebody said, 'Know, Mr Bell, I sometimes thought that you represented to adults all the things in young people that they disliked, and to young people, all the things in adults that they disliked. [*Everyone laughs.*]

LAUREN   That's beautiful.

SMITHA   That's lovely.

JOHN   I think that ... the kind of the fearless, the happy and the trouble all came together in that job. Though I do, I think, you know, I've got a friend, she worked with us for twenty years. She's my closest female friend and, you know, we laugh so much. And she, I know she has a very different background from me. She came to ... alcoholic parents and she came to faith in a mission hall when she was 17.

But she just sees God as one who intrinsically intends us for happiness! And that, you know, droll religion and boredom, particularly liturgical boredom [*Smitha and Lauren laugh*] is a sin against the Holy Ghost! And it's not that we should be telling new jokes so everybody's ... But, the sense of being complete in yourself, and despite all that has happened, I can stand here, I know who I am and I know whose I am. And I'm happy with that.

SMITHA   I was going to say, there's a funny sketch with Mr Bean – this is going back a while – singing Hallelujah, but you know, he's ... he's sitting in church and he's falling asleep! [*John and Lauren laugh.*] Um, and I just want people to wake up when I preach, actually! [*John and Lauren laugh.*] I want people to shout for joy when they come to church because this is abundant and this is good for the soul; it's good for the body ...

LAUREN   Yeah!

SMITHA   ... and it's good for us together. I think that's what it is.

LAUREN   I wonder if we haven't lost that sort of playfulness, the sense of wonder, the excitement about it all, the sort of looking through child's eyes and thinking like, 'Whoa', like we get access to this, these miracles, these unimaginable things, this beautiful creation, you know, we, we're very grown up about it all.

JOHN   People keep saying, you know, the British or the English and certainly the Scots are kind of, you know, a bit restrained.

LAUREN   Oh, I don't think the Scots are restrained. English, yes. I've never seen a restrained Scot! [*Everybody laughs.*]

JOHN   I remember going to a Black church in London and I was told, you know, before, if you've ever been in there, people will, will shout things. So I said, 'I'm so happy to be here – Hallelujah!' And then we're going, 'Praise the Lord!' and all this is happening ... And then it came to the point where there was the giving of the offering and it was an offering of money. And then this old man got up and he said, I'm ... today I've been asked if I'll lay my gift on the altar and my gift today is a gift of song. And then he says ...

LAUREN   Yes!

JOHN   Oh, uh, I've forgotten the tune. And this woman shouts, 'Hallelujah!' So, he just sat back down, and later I said, I said to her, 'Why is it when that old man forgot the tune you shouted, "Hallelujah"?' She said, 'Because he's a lousy singer.' [*Everyone laughs.*]

But there was in that church, you know, a depth of faith and, to some extent, a fearlessness in that congregation, who had had to deal with quite a hard time. But also, there was this kind of joy.

SMITHA   We need to be fearless in our questioning, in our fears and our doubts, and to be able to articulate it actually, to say, I don't know what I don't know.

LAUREN   Yeah …!

SMITHA   Do you know what this means, or can you help me? And I think quite often people in churches, church communities, are scared to say that they don't know.

JOHN   That's an interesting thing. It's a fear of inadequacy.

SMITHA   Yes. Yeah. And maybe sort of *guilt* because they don't know. Maybe they didn't sit up and learn everything they needed to in Sunday school because that seems to be the only place where people learn and then the exit track is confirmation … And then people discover, maybe because they hadn't quite got the big picture, or a picture where they saw God as God is, that they come back to faith, that they come back with their questions, but that it is okay, whether you have stayed within an in group or have wandered away or whatever, to ask questions, which are searching questions, which are burning questions, or sometimes stupid, ignorant questions, *you think*!

LAUREN   I've got one I can confess … 'cause we had a little chat before we started and sort of roughly what we were going to talk about. And so, spoiler alert, for people watching, but at some point you're going to ask us about Incarnation. And I thought, gosh, I better Google it. [*John and Smith laugh.*] I didn't know. It's one of those things, you *know*, but if somebody puts you on camera and says, 'What does that word mean to you?' there's a part of me that was like, 'Oh, I really better be sure I, I really know, not just think I know.'

JOHN   No, that's, that's very helpful …

SMITHA   Oh, can you just tell me what it is?

LAUREN   It's the coming to life, like of a deity. It's the, yeah. Can I … John will sign that off.

JOHN   We're going to come to it! What I'm feeling for is

whether there's also a sense in which, if we're called in any way to be fearless, then that also means that, in the image of Jesus taking a stand on that which is clearly wrong, and not being afraid to deal with issues which are awkward. Because if the truth makes us whole, why should we deal with half-truths or lies?

Now, you know, I'm not great at this at all, but I think of ... There was an occasion when I felt genuinely called to talk about child sex abuse. It was a Greenbelt talk, which I gave. And, I think the reason was partly because I knew a lot ... a number of people, who had been the victims of it. But I was aware that the church never *speaks* about this.

I mean, we have the, all these kind of, uh, mechanisms by which we try to keep safeguarding, but what do you do and why does this happen? And why does it happen in religious circles? And I did some preparation and then ... and I realized that there were no books or very few books about this in Britain. I would have to get books from abroad. And I thought, if I got books from America, where some publications have been made, and they get opened, they might think that I'm into this. So, I got my secretary to get them, and all the rest of it. But I remember, the more I kind of struggled and prayed with it, the more I thought, we have to deal with this.

And, you know, at Greenbelt there's this huge, big tents and ... the place was packed, and normally people would be shouting. It was like going into a crematorium. And all the way, while I spoke, people were weeping. You know, they had brought their experience and nobody hitherto had actually articulated the degree of it, the frequency of it, and ask the questions about how do we prevent this from happening and how do we deal both with the victim, and with the perpetrator.

And I also thought, nothing in my faith formation had prepared me to do this, but rather I'd been encouraged to keep to that which was safe. Now, I'm not making an issue of my own experience. But I just wonder whether you've either been called to be fearless in the face of something which is really quite troubling.

SMITHA   I think, really, we're living through challenging times. We're talking about peace, for example, in a war-torn world. What does that peace mean in a context where people are not talking to each other, or certainly not willing to work for the hard-won peace, where we can hear each other, where inhabiting a church where you say you were ill equipped to talk about child abuse, which is a feature, sadly, of our churches ...

But there's so much more that's going on in our world – modern slavery, human trafficking, human trafficking at a rate which is *untold* right now. And it's costing the lives of women and children worldwide. But there is money to be made, and this is lucrative business. We should be speaking out and about and up for the people.

Racism is another, you know, people turn a blind eye. But actually, we must speak out *against* the sin of racism, in our churches, in our society, and equip people for the best ways to intervene, to show allyship, to say, 'This is wrong.' I think that's what you said?

JOHN   Well, and also you mentioned in the passing, we don't talk about money.

SMITHA   We don't.

JOHN   Your money is what allegedly makes the world go round. From Genesis to Revelation, all through the prophets, through the letters and in the life of Jesus, money is not an issue which is avoided. I mean, he talks about money and yet within Christian circles, we don't talk about, we don't ... as if money is an inherently evil thing.

LAUREN   Yeah.

JOHN   And I think if you demonise money, rather than look at the potential when it's best used, then it becomes an embarrassment for Christian people.

LAUREN   I think it might be the most misquoted. I'm sure there are others, but you know, the root of all evil is *love* of money, rather than the money itself, isn't it?

I think *no* conversation should be off the table with Jesus at the centre; absolutely none. There's no part of this world that Jesus isn't aware, God isn't aware, is happening. And yes, there are sort of dark corners and there are, there are things happening, which are horrific and are *so contrary* to Jesus' will for us as people and his world.

But actually, we need to bring it into the light. And I commend you for standing up and speaking about something which is, which so many people would rather brush under the carpet. And also to be a woman of colour who stands up and talks about racism when there are people who go, 'Oh, she's moaning. It's not a problem.' You know, Oh, I can't just say ... It's hard. And you *must* be fearless. And to an extent, you know, I do feel like, particularly anytime I've spoken about something contentious, God has kind of put a veil over me so that if someone's mean about me or criticises me, you know, it doesn't touch the sides in a way that, certainly when I was younger and less spiritually mature and things, it really would have.

But this is *important*. And if people can't hear it in church or at a Christian festival or in a preach or a podcast or run by Christian leaders who are safe hands, who understand God's heart and the Bible, they're going to find out about it somewhere else. If they can't learn about sex from Christians, they'll watch pornography.

You know, we can intercept, we can show what God's design was supposed to bring us before they're contorted. Or we can stay silent and let people see where the world takes them.

JOHN	This is the lovely thing. This is what the Incarnation is about, you know, that God is not silent in these things. And I think that the word Incarnation, which now I love, *profoundly* love, is a word which has become a bit of kind of theological jargon and people, you know, yourself, you know ...
LAUREN	Shall I give you the official definition?
JOHN	Oh, tell us. Tell us the definition.

LAUREN A person who embodies in flesh a deity, spirit or quality.

JOHN Well, there you are.

LAUREN According to the internet.

JOHN According to the internet. But according, according to, according to God, when God becomes human in Jesus, all of human life is lit up with a potential of great glory and transformation. And the Incarnation is not the babyfest at Bethlehem. The Incarnation is happening when Jesus heals people.

The Incarnation is happening when Jesus chastises people who set up a tax regime, which inflicts poverty on those who are poorest. The Incarnation is happening when Jesus engages with people of different cultures as if they were his own culture, because there's no difference. And this is the permeation of God through all of society. It's a bigger God than the baby who lies in the manger.

SMITHA Absolutely. And it's the call to that bigger God, which will be about food justice, economic justice, political justice, you know, justice at every level. Because God in Jesus is calling out those injustices. God in Jesus has come to be the way, the truth and the life. To show the way. To help *us* to speak out the truth and therefore to liberate. So, it's incredible. It's our task.

JOHN I know, it's our task and it's our time, sadly. [*Smitha and Lauren laugh.*] And, eh, I want to thank you on behalf of my two friends, and myself for the joy of being able to share this with you. We hope that you have enjoyed this series. And we hope you enjoy Advent and Christmas. And may God bless you all. Bye-bye

NOTES

SESSION 1 ADVENT – A TIME FOR THE KIDS?

1 R. Albert Mohler Jr, *The Apostles' Creed: Discovering Authentic Christianity in an Age of Counterfeits* (Nashville, TN: Thomas Nelson, 2020), p. 121.
2 J. I. Packer, *Affirming the Apostles' Creed* (Carol Stream, IL: Crossway, 2008), p. 7.
3 Nicole Kidman, on her Facebook page, 12 October 2016.
4 George Bernard Shaw, Preface to *Androcles and the Lion: On the Prospects of Christianity* (1912). Public domain.
5 Cecil Frances Alexander (1818–95), 'Once in Royal David's City', *Hymns for Little Children* (London: J. Masters & Co, 1888). Public domain.
6 Rob Bell, *Velvet Elvis: Repainting the Christian Faith* (Grand Rapids, MI: Zondervan, 2006), p. 25.
7 Leonardo Boff, *Jesus Christ Liberator* (London: SPCK, 1979), p. 50.
8 Isaac Hutchings, copyright WGRG, The Iona Community (2003).
9 Bruce J. Malina and Richard L. Rohrbaugh, *Social-Science Commentary on the Synoptic Gospels* (Minneapolis, MN: Fortress Press, 1989), pp. 84 and 211.

SESSION 2 THE LIFE OMITTED

1 Keith Getty in Keith Getty and Stuart Townend, 'Finding a New Song, Biblically Speaking', *Worship Leader magazine*, September 2010.
2 John Betjeman, *Sweet Songs of Zion*, ed. Stephen Games (London: John Murray, 2007), p. 21.
3 *The Church Hymnary* (London: Henry Frowde, 1898).
4 *The English Hymnal* (Oxford: Oxford University Press, 1906).
5 *Redemption Songs* (Glasgow: Pickering and Inglis, 1900).
6 Ernesto Cardenal, *The Gospels in Art by the Peasants of Solentiname* (Maryknoll, NY: Orbis Books, 1984), p. 6.
7 C. H. Dodd, *History and the Gospel* (Claremont, CA: Pomona Press, 2007), pp. 90–101.
8 Louis FitzGerald Benson (1855–1930), 'O Sing a Song of Bethlehem'.
9 Sydney Carter, 'Lord of the Dance', 1963. Words and music: Stainer & Bell Ltd.
10 Katie Geneva Canon, *Inheriting Our Mothers' Gardens* (London: Westminster Press, 1988), p. 74.
11 Dietrich Bonhoeffer, *The Cost of Discipleship* (London: SCM Press, 1959), p. 50.
12 St Augustine, trans. E. B. Pusey, *The Confessions: Book X* (AD 401). Public domain.
13 Here is a reproduction of Salvador Dali's painting, *Christ of John of the Cross*, https://artuk.org/discover/artworks/christ-of-st-john-of-the-cross-83704 (accessed 1 May 2024).
14 Edwin Morgan, 'Salvador Dali: Christ of St John of the Cross', *A Book of Lives* (Manchester: Carcanet, 2007), available at: https://www.scottishpoetrylibrary.org.uk/poem/salvador-dali-christ-st-john-cross/ (accessed 1 May 2024). Copyright © Edwin Morgan 2007. Reproduced with permission of the Licensor through PLSclear.
15 Isaiah 53:3, Colossians 1:19.
16 Stephen Schwartz, '"We Even Performed It in Front of the Pope!" – How We Made *Godspell*', *The Guardian*, 10 May 2021.
17 Damian Carrington, 'Revealed: the Huge Climate Impact of the Middle Classes', *The Guardian*, 20 November 2023.
18 Global Justice, 'Ending Corporate Impunity', (n.d.), https://www.globaljustice.org.uk/our-campaigns/climate/ending-corporate-impunity/ (accessed 1 May 2024).

19 Jarrid Wilson, *Jesus Swagger: Break Free from Poser Christianity* (Nashville, TN: Thomas Nelson, 2015), p. 9.

20 Evelyn Miranda-Feliciano in William A. Dyrness, *Emerging Voices in Global Christian Theology* (Grand Rapids, MI: Zondervan, 1994), p. 158.

21 Marilynne Robinson, *When I Was a Child I Read Books* (London: Virago, 2013), pp. 136–7. Reproduced with permission of the Licensor through PLSclear.

SESSION 3 UNSPOKEN IN ADVENT

1 Martin Luther, quoted in Justo L. González, *The Story of Christianity: The Reformation to the Present Day*, rev. and updated (New York: HarperOne, 2010), vol. 2, p. 25.

2 James Merritt, *52 Weeks with Jesus: Fall in Love with the One Who Changed Everything* (Eugene, OR: Harvest House, 2015), p. 27.

3 Frederick Buechner, *Peculiar Treasures* (New York: Harper & Row, 1979), p. 145.

4 Albert Nolan, *Jesus Before Christianity* (Maryknoll, NY: Orbis, 1992), p. 78.

5 Sarah Bessey, *Jesus Feminist: An Invitation to Revisit the Bible's View of Women* (Brentwood, TN: Howard Books, 2013), p. 92.

6 Dorothy L. Sayers, *Are Women Human?* (Grand Rapids, MI: Eerdmans, 1971), p. 47.

7 John 4:1–42.

8 Rebecca McLaughlin, *Jesus through the Eyes of Women: How the First Female Disciples Help Us Know and Love the Lord* (Carol Stream, IL: Crossway / The Gospel Coalition, 2022), p. 84.

9 Brendan Lehane, *Early Celtic Christianity* (London: Constable, 1995), p. 104.

10 *The Women's Bible Commentary* (Louisville, KY: Westminster John Knox Press, 1992), p. 254.

11 Elisabeth Schüssler Fiorenza, *But She Said: Feminist Practices of Biblical Interpretation* (Boston, MA: Beacon Press, 1992), p. 97.

12 2 Kings 5:1–14.

13 Luke 17:11–19.

14 Luke 7:1–10.

15 Bessey, *Jesus Feminist*, p. 4.

SESSION 4 A LIFE OF RISK

1 Plato, *Republic*, Book III, available at: https://www.perseus.tufts.edu/hopper/ (accessed 1 May 2024).

2 Victor Hugo, *William Shakespeare: Book 2*, trans. A. Baillot (Boston, MA: Estes and Lauriat, 1864), chapter 4. In the original: 'Ce qu'on ne peut dire et ce qu'on ne peut taire, la musique l'exprime.' Available at: https://www.gutenberg.org/files/53490/53490-h/53490-h.htm (accessed 1 May 2024).

3 John Wilson, 1991.

4 William Barclay, *The Gospel of Luke* (Louisville, KY: Westminster John Knox Press, 2001), p. 92.

5 N. T. Wright, *What Saint Paul Really Said: Was Paul of Tarsus the Real Founder of Christianity?* (Grand Rapids, MI: Eerdmans, 1997), p. 36.

6 Rebecca McLaughlin, *Jesus through the Eyes of Women: How the First Female Disciples Help Us Know and Love the Lord* (Carol Stream, IL: Crossway / The Gospel Coalition, 2022), p. 17.

7 John V. Taylor, *The Christlike God* (London: SCM Press, 1992), p. 135.

8 John O'Donohue, *Anam Cara: Spiritual Wisdom from the Celtic World* (New York: Bantam Books, 2011), p. 76.

9 This section is copyright WGRG, The Iona Community (2022).

10 Donald M. Baillie, *God was in Christ* (London: Faber, 1956), p. 151.

JOHN L. BELL is a member of the Iona Community and an ordained minister, and for twenty years was a contributor to BBC Radio 4's 'Thought for the Day'. Over many years, he has consistently been one of the biggest draws at the Greenbelt Festival, and his work as a teacher and speaker takes him frequently into Eastern Europe, Asia, Africa, Australia and North America. In 2018, John received from Archbishop Justin Welby The Thomas Cranmer Award for Worship for his outstanding Christian witness, through hymn-writing, broadcasting and social action.

SMITHA PRASADAM is Bishop of Huddersfield and comes from a family of pioneers and missionaries. She is the first woman from India to be consecrated bishop; her mother was the first to be ordained priest in the Church of England.

LAUREN WINDLE is a speaker and journalist, published by *Vogue*, *MailOnline*, *HuffPost*, *Red* magazine, *Marie Claire*, *The Sun* and many more. https://laurenwindle.com

York Courses: https://spckpublishing.co.uk/bible-studies-and-group-resources/york-courses